UNDERSTANDING
ESL
WRITERS

A Guide for Teachers

ILONA LEKI

University of Tennessee

Boynton/Cook Publishers
HEINEMANN
Portsmouth, New Hampshire

Boynton/Cook Publishers Inc.
A subsidiary of Reed Elsevier Inc.
361 Hanover Street   Portsmouth, NH 03801-3912
Offices and agents throughout the world

Every effort has been made to contact the copyright holders for permission to reprint
borrowed material. We regret any oversights that may have occurred
and would be happy to rectify them in future printings.

Library of Congress Cataloging-in-Publication Data

Leki, Ilona.
    Understanding ESL writers : a guide for teachers / Ilona Leki.
        p.   cm.
    Includes bibliographical references (p.   ).
    ISBN 0-86709-303-X
    1. English language—Study and teaching—Foreign speakers.
    2. English language—Composition and exercises—Study and teaching.
    3. English language—Rhetoric—Study and teaching.   I. Title.
    PE1128.A2L385   1992
    808'.042'07—dc20   91-35814
                                                                    CIP

Cover designed by T. Watson Bogaard
Printed in the United States of America

99 98 97 96   5 6 7 8

UNDERSTANDING ESL WRITERS

A Guide for Teachers

This book is lovingly dedicated to Nina Leki and to our family's wonderful memories of John H. Leki.

Contents

Preface

Around the world some 1.4 billion people are learning and using English as a second language. International student enrollment at U.S. colleges and universities reached the all-time high of 407,500 in 1990/91. Writing classrooms in these institutions are the locus of a difficult struggle for these non-native English-speaking students. They live with the contradiction that although it takes time to learn English well and time to learn to write well, they do not have much time. Their voices may be muffled, or silenced, by their lack of English skills. Yet many who teach these students remain committed, in the words of Barbara Kroll, to a pedagogy of inclusiveness, diversity, and enfranchisement.

I am indebted to my friends and colleagues whose commitment to that pedagogy has been an inspiration to me. I would like to thank Barbara Warren, Kirsten Benson, Joy Reid, Tony Silva, and Ken Tunnell for giving their time so generously in reading, commenting on, and offering suggestions for earlier drafts of this book; Joan Carson and Tony Silva for their unwavering encouragement; Barbara Kroll for her generous collegiality; Norman Sanders and Bob Leggett of the English department at the University of Tennessee, whose support won me a Hodges Research Award, allowing me to work on this book; Bob Boynton for his interest in the project; Alan Huisman for his patient and efficient help with the manuscript of this book; and all the rest of the staff at Boynton/Cook and Heinemann for consistently making my work easier. Finally, I want to thank my Mom and the rest of my family for their love and belief in me, Pete and Debbie for the hours of phone conversations about ESL and other such political issues, Bob and Sue, Ray and Cindy, and most especially Ken, for always keeping the joy in my life.

Introduction

This book is for writing teachers looking for guidance toward understanding students who are non-native speakers of English. It is also for future teachers of English as a Second Language (ESL), teacher trainees in graduate programs who have not had much contact with ESL students and would like an introduction to some of their special characteristics, qualities, and situations.

Teaching writing to ESL students is not radically different from teaching writing to native English speakers. Many of the same attitudes, techniques, and even syllabuses work well with ESL students. Teachers who find ESL students in their classes for the first time and who are worried about meeting these students' special needs already know a great deal about the best way to help them improve their writing.

But ESL students are different from native students, and in ways not necessarily predictable for teachers who have not spent much time thinking about or working with them. Sometimes these unpredictable differences cause anxiety and misunderstanding. Colleagues of mine newly exposed to second language students have expressed a variety of concerns: Will I be able to understand what they say? Will they be able to understand me? Will they be able to participate in group activities with the other students? Will I have to lower my standards in evaluating their work? Will I inadvertently say things they will find culturally offensive? They have worried out loud about the extra time and attention they fear ESL students will require and about the inadequacy of their preparation to deal with these students' needs.

The purpose of this book is to help make teaching writing to non-natives easier and more enjoyable and to aid writing teachers in deciding among methodologies, textbooks, and suggestions for teaching ESL students. I have tried to make the book interesting and readable by referring whenever possible to my own experiences and those of my colleagues who teach ESL students.

A word about the term ESL: I refer to these students as ESL or second language (L2) students, but these names do not always reflect reality, since for many of these students, English is not a second, but a third, fourth, or fifth language. Furthermore, I am using the term here to cover both international students, who usually come to an English-speaking country to study for a limited period of time, and immigrant students who have come to stay for at least the foreseeable future. Differences between these groups of students are addressed in the course of the book, but their experiences also bind them together in important ways, especially for the writing teacher.

The first section of the book briefly explains the history of ESL writing instruction and describes models of second language acquisition. With this background writing teachers can better understand the previous instruction in writing some ESL students may have had and the social and cognitive dimensions of the task that confronts these students as they function in a foreign language environment.

The second section of the book focuses on the students in all their diversity. Although institutions may group them with basic writers for the sake of convenience, ESL students are often not basic writers at all, but experienced writers with a developing mastery of English. Chapter 3 reviews some of the differences in attitude and experience between basic writers, second dialect learners, and ESL students. Chapters 4 and 5 discuss the varying educational, political, economic, and cultural backgrounds ESL students bring to our educational institutions and their expectations of living and studying in the United States. We see them primarily as students in our classes, but these chapters are intended to provide a glimpse of the real people behind the role of writing students — their fears, excitement, motivations, disappointments, and successes in dealing with their new environment. These chapters should be of special interest to future ESL teachers.

The last section of the book is devoted to the writing behaviors of ESL students. Chapter 6 deals with writing assignments: what students are likely to expect as assignments, what they might select to write about, and what kinds of assignments may cause them trouble. Chapter 7 reviews what we currently know about the composing processes of second language writers, how they differ from those of first language writers, and how they are similar. It also includes information about students' own perceptions of what it is like to write in a language not yet entirely their own.

Chapter 8 deals with contrastive rhetoric, that is, the different ways in which cultures choose to arrange information and express ideas in writing. Although these choices function appropriately within their own cultures, culture-bound assumptions about writing cannot always cross linguistic and cultural barriers. ESL students may bring with them practices and ideas about writing which do not mirror our own and which are all the more problematic because they function unconsciously, as a felt sense of how a piece of writing should go. This chapter specifically addresses the assumptions of a few cultures representative of the ESL student population.

The issue of errors, finally though inevitably, appears in Chapter 9. For some teachers, particularly those unaccustomed to reading the writing of ESL students, errors are the most salient feature of their work. This chapter attempts to give the current view of language errors prevalent among ESL professionals, indicating what errors imply about language learning and where some of these errors may originate. It ends with a catalog of typical errors made by ESL writers and possible sources of those errors.

The last chapter addresses the issue of how to respond to the writing of ESL students, to both the content and the formal features of their writing. Here writing teachers will find themselves on familiar ground, since much of what is appropriate for native English-speaking students also helps ESL student writers. This chapter discusses the question of how far writing teachers, institutions, and the students themselves can reasonably expect to get in improving ESL student writing and offers suggestions for appropriate responses.

In the conclusion, I try to derive from the content of the book a brief summary of what seems to me reasonable advice to give a writing teacher unsure of how to deal with non-native writers.

This book surely does not answer all questions or anticipate all problems writing teachers may confront with second language writers. But it was written with the conviction and knowledge that ESL students have a great deal to bring to our educational institutions and to our native students. They are enormous resources for mixed native/non-native English classes, bringing with them glimpses of worlds our native students may never have the opportunity to see. Attempting to understand the backgrounds, motivations, and assumptions of other peoples will help the young people of this country realize that they do not live alone on this earth but must share it with others whose agendas may differ from their own.

This book was guided and inspired by respect and sympathy not only for the teachers who work with the writing of non-native students but perhaps even more for the students engaged in the thrilling and at times frightening experience of going after education in a strange country and in a language which is not, as yet, entirely their own.

SECTION I

THE BACKGROUND

Chapter One

History of Writing Instruction in English as a Second Language

For the moment let us note that getting the better of words in writing is commonly a very hard struggle. And I am thinking now of words which are in one's own language. The struggle is all the greater when they are not.

H. G. Widdowson

Imagine you are in a classroom in which the medium of instruction is the language you know the best after English. You are asked to write in that L2 (second language) for fifteen minutes, exploring your thoughts on a subject the teacher designates. You are to write continuously, not worrying about grammar or spelling, just trying to get thoughts down on paper. Can you do it? What kinds of obstacles do you experience as you attempt to get ideas that you have in your mind into that L2? Are you writing at your usual speed? Are you thinking in English and trying to translate into your L2 or are you trying to think in the L2? Are you having trouble finding words? Are you having trouble even thinking of ideas? When you finish, you are to go back and read what you have written. Does your free-writing sample accurately reflect your thoughts on the subject? Does it reflect your usual subtlety and

3

acuity of thought? If the teacher suddenly told you that you could continue this free-writing exercise in English, what changes would be evident in the continuation of your text?

If writing in an L1 (first language) requires the orchestration of countless skills and strategies, from the most basic motor skills to the most complex cognitive strategies, writing in an L2 clearly increases the writer's cognitive load. Furthermore, the social complexity of a writing task also expands. In most writing contexts, the writer must in some sense invent the reader, imagining what the reader might contribute to the communication to clarify meaning, where the reader might stop, puzzled at something in the text, and have to ask for a restatement or an elaboration. This is true of most written communication, but for an L2 writer, this task is much more difficult. The reader is a real stranger, someone from another culture with a different understanding of distinctions like relevant/irrelevant, logical/illogical, someone who has a very different, culturally determined sense of what constitutes proof of an argument, what an argument is, who may construct an argument, and even who may write. If inexperienced native English-speaking writers need to learn to distinguish clearly, for example, between what is relevant and what is irrelevant, how much greater the problem becomes when the writer is not a native of this culture.

Writing: The Last Language Skill

Despite the considerable challenge confronting non-native writers, recognition of the nature of that challenge, even by teachers of English as a Second Language (ESL), was slow in coming. Before the 1960s, most ESL classes were linked to citizenship classes for immigrants, focusing on indoctrinating the immigrants into what were perceived as the glories of freedom and opportunity in their new home by teaching enough oral language skills and reading to permit these aspirants to pass the citizenship exam and then, typically, to become fodder in the industrial cannon through low-paying, unskilled jobs, often in factories. These factory jobs required few literacy skills, and thus the ESL students in English classes were assumed to have little need for writing skills.

This political rationale for underplaying the importance of writing in English moved in step with linguistic notions about language and language pedagogies prevailing before the 1960s. After World War II, interest in Skinnerian behaviorism (1957) as a theoretical base for language learning soared, and the audio-lingual method (ALM), rooted in behaviorist theories, was the dominant language teaching methodology. Drawing from the writings of Swiss linguist Ferdinand de Saussure and the structuralist linguists, ALM viewed spoken language as primary, with writing last in the order of language skills to be learned (Fries, 1945). Even when ESL classes included a writing component, writing in the language class was primarily used to reinforce what students had learned to say (Rivers, 1968). Writing transcribed speech; it was not used to create, to express ideas, to synthesize information, to explore thoughts.

With the post-Sputnik influx of "foreign students" to the United States in the 1960s, the English-teaching mission expanded to include preparing these non-native students to function in institutions of higher education. This meant teaching them to write extended prose for academic purposes (Kaplan, 1988). Nevertheless, the language teachers who undertook to prepare these students for university level writing continued to operate under the influence of a structuralist view of language. Language was imagined as a complex of small, easily digestible bits of grammar, which students could master one at a time, adding each new bit to those already under control. Learning to write, then, consisted of practicing bits of language in sentence patterns, striving for grammatical perfection. Concerned not to overload students' capacity to learn these grammatical patterns, teachers had students focus on one part of the writing task at a time and prepared carefully guided composition activities in which, for example, students might manipulate a text by changing all singulars to plurals, or all male pronouns to female pronouns, and making all other necessary, related grammatical changes (Paulston and Dykstra, 1973). But students rarely created texts themselves, and the content of those texts that were generated by the student writers was typically considered incidental to the practice of sentence or rhetorical patterns (Finocchiaro, 1974). Teaching writing was, in fact, teaching formalities of language.

Unfortunately, it soon became clear that even if students were able to do grammar-based guided compositions, and even if students did have a fairly good grasp of grammar, they still produced peculiar, non-English-sounding texts when asked to write even somewhat more creatively. To help students get beyond the sentence level, writing teachers had students extend their previous exercises on accumulating bits of language to form sentence patterns; students now learned to combine sentence patterns to form paragraphs and paragraphs to form whole essays (Bander, 1971). This application of sentence-level practice to paragraphs and then to full essays was aided by the birth of the study of contrastive rhetoric, which surmised that each culture has a manner of presenting ideas particular to itself, just as each language has a syntax particular to itself (Kaplan,

1966). In the oldest and most simplistic application of the findings of contrastive rhetoric, writing teachers would determine paragraph patterns typical of English and teach those to their ESL students. The students imitated the patterns, assuming that by learning these basic patterns, they would then be able to transfer these skills to the writing of acceptable academic prose and pour their writing content into the carefully prepared and practiced molds. The patterns taught to ESL students were the traditional ones taught to native English-speaking freshman writers in academic institutions: a paragraph consists of a topic sentence, three supporting sentences, and a concluding sentence; an essay consists of an introductory paragraph with a thesis statement at the end of it, followed by three paragraphs of development, followed by a concluding paragraph.

Process Approaches to Teaching ESL Writing

But, while teachers of native-speaker writing classes gradually moved away from this rigidity, ESL teachers, who were essentially language teachers, not writing teachers, stayed with the approach longer, finally moving away in the early 1980s. In the 1970s the ESL profession generally began abandoning structuralist views of language and grammar-based methodologies in favor of approaches which focused on communication, not grammatical accuracy, as the goal of language learning (Savignon, 1972). ESL teachers and researchers especially interested in writing also shifted their perspective and began to examine native-speaker writing classes, already well engaged in the paradigm shift toward a process approach to teaching writing (Hairston, 1982; Zamel, 1976). In the 1980s increasing numbers of ESL conference papers explored the idea of using process approaches with ESL students.

Nevertheless, while various techniques and even attitudes which characterize process approach classrooms have found their way into ESL writing classes, the impact of the process approach has been limited by several factors. First, until recently few ESL teachers received any particular training in teaching writing and even now few graduate ESL programs include separate courses in teaching writing (MacDonald and Hall, 1990). Thus, ESL and EFL (English as a Foreign Language, i.e., usually English taught outside of English-speaking countries) teachers may not be as aware of non-traditional approaches to teaching writing. Furthermore, most ESL teachers are in fact primarily language teachers. This may be especially true in language institutes throughout the English-speaking world and even more so among the thousands of ESL/EFL teachers in non-English-speaking countries. These teachers would be less likely to abandon more traditional views of teaching writing and more likely to resist the de-emphasis on grammar characteristic of process methodologies.

Finally, certain process approaches have been criticized by teachers/researchers of both native and non-native writers for focusing too insistently on personal experience, on finding and developing a personal voice in writing (Horowitz, 1986b; Faigley, 1989). The emphasis on writing about personal experience poses particular problems for some ESL students not accustomed to focusing on themselves in their writing (see Chapter 6, "Writing Behaviors"). Process approaches to teaching writing are further accused of giving ESL students the unrealistic impression that grammatical accuracy is not important (Eskey, 1983). In addition, with its emphasis on multiple drafts, the process approach is said to fail to prepare ESL students for the demands of the academic essay exam with its single draft restrictions (Horowitz, 1986b). Finally, some ESL writing specialists fear that the humanistic bias of the process approach may give ESL students false perceptions of their own abilities and unrealistic expectations of success in college-level writing assignments (Horowitz, 1986b).

Writing English for Special Purposes

At more or less the same time as process approaches to teaching writing were being explored by ESL writing teachers, another movement grew in L2 writing classes: interest in English for Special Purposes, English for Science and Technology, or English for Academic Purposes. This interest reflects certain clear realities for L2 writers. First, unlike L1 writers who will need to write for many different purposes within their own society, many L2 writers will return to their native countries and may find very little need to write again in English at all, and certainly little need to write the kind of self-reflective, self-exploratory essay that was seen as typifying process classrooms (Horowitz, 1986b). Second, the self-reflection taught in process approach classes functions in part to socialize young native students into their own society, to help them situate themselves in current social and political debates, and thereby to prepare them to take up various roles in this society. But such goals are not appropriate for ESL students who are unlikely to remain in this society. Arguably, to maintain that developing a capacity for introspection in writing is *universally* appropriate is an ethnocentric position which divorces socialization from specific societies; interest in developing individual voice is not necessarily shared worldwide. The cultural imperialism argument aside, it is also argued that the time ESL students spend in English-speaking countries is too short to allow them to indulge in training along lines marginal to their main pursuits (Johns, 1991; Huckin and Olsen, 1984). Thus, if ESL students are going to learn to write in English, the writing should be related to their major field of study, which for many ESL students is likely to be business, agriculture, or scientific and engineering technologies (Horowitz, 1986a). The proponents of English for Special/Academic Purposes maintain that ESL students studying in English-speaking institutions must be prepared for the actual uses they will eventually make of their ability to write in English, that is, for their classes (essay exams, lab reports, and so forth) and for their continued participation in their academic field after they graduate and return to their own countries. (For challenges to these arguments, see Liebman-Kleine, 1986; Hamp-Lyons, 1986; and particularly, Spack, forthcoming, who argues that academic writing does not begin in dispassionate objectivity, but rather in passionate personal engagement with a topic.)

Conclusion

At this point in the early 1990s, the debate about the most appropriate way to teach writing to ESL students centers around these two positions, a generalized initiation into the academic discourse community much like that provided for native English-speaking students or a more narrow and focused ESP/EAP approach (Johns, 1991; Spack, 1988). (For a fuller description of the history of ESL writing, see Silva, 1990.) The importance of the debate for non-ESL writing teachers, and the importance of this brief history of ESL writing instruction, lies in the fact that non-ESL writing teachers with ESL students in their classes may find that their students' development as writers has been affected by shifts in the ESL profession and debates about these shifts. Students coming from a traditional orientation may feel uncomfortable with an emphasis on self-examination and self-revelation through writing. They may expect quite a bit more grammar than writing teachers are interested in covering. They may not be accustomed to sharing their writing with classmates, may at first be unwilling to accept peer corrections, or may feel intensely agitated with a non-instrumental approach to teaching writing, that is, a non-technical writing approach. It is also important to keep in mind that unlike L1 writing students, many L2 writing students are still studying the English language, not only learning to write but learning to read, listen, and speak in English.

In addition, they are learning to make their way through many aspects of North American society, including its educational system. If native students experience culture shock as they enter colleges throughout their own country, the experience is geometrically intensified for students facing acculturation struggles at all levels of existence, including climate and food.

Finally, in teaching writing to ESL students, it is important to re-examine the goals of the writing class. From the point of view of the institution in which the writing classes take place, what are the institutional goals set for ESL writing students? are these goals appropriate? what do teachers in content classes expect of ESL students' writing? what is the purpose of having ESL students in writing classes or even studying at these institutions? From the teacher's point of view, what are our goals as teachers for these students? are they the same as the goals we set for native English-speaking students? should they be? And, most importantly, from the student's point of view, what are the goals of the individual ESL students taking writing courses? For reasons of their personal language-learning histories or their social and educational backgrounds, their goals may be seriously in conflict with our own. If their goals are to write without error and our goals for them are that they learn to write honestly, that they discover their own voices, both our task and theirs may become exceedingly difficult. If we need to teach writers rather than to teach writing (Rose, 1989; Zamel, 1985), we need to know who those writers are and what their goals might be.

Chapter Two

Models of Second Language Acquisition

The most obvious and consequential distinguishing characteristic of ESL writers is that their writing occurs in their second (or third or fourth) language. Yet in certain ways theories about and insights into second language acquisition may be useful for all writing teachers, since writing researchers, theorists, and teachers have pointed out that even in one's native language, learning to write is something like learning a second language (Freedman, Pringle, and Yalden, 1983). No one is a "native speaker" of writing. For the most part, everyone learns to write at school, not naturally as a simple result of interactions with others as is the case in first language acquisition.

To begin to understand the specific difficulties of L2 writing students, it may be useful to know something about how people are thought to learn second languages. I have not tried to be complete in this discussion of second language acquisition theories and models, but rather, I have selected issues and L2 acquisition models which seem to bear on teaching L2 writing. Although it may seem counter-intuitive, researchers do not spend much time considering which specific first and second languages are involved in L2 acquisition. They concede that to function fluently in English may take a native speaker of Chinese longer than, for example, a native speaker of French, but the same processes are involved for the learner regardless of the languages involved. Some of the basic questions L2 acquisition researchers pose center on the nature of the L2 input the learner gets and the learner's personal and cognitive profile.

Issues in L2 Acquisition

In learning a second language, the learner obviously must be exposed to the language to be learned, the target language. The input may be formal or informal; it may be oral or written. The nature of the input will have an effect on how the learner internalizes the L2. For example, L2 writers whose input has been informal oral language, as is the case for many immigrant L2 writers, may be able to hold conversations with native speakers but may experience particular problems in adjusting to the demands of academic writing. Cummins (1979) distinguishes between two types of language acquisition: Basic Interpersonal Communicative Skills (BICS) and Cognitive Academic Language Proficiency (CALP). L2 students quite proficient in BICS may be unable to survive in an environment, like an academic environment, which demands proficiency in CALP. The reverse may also be true, of course. That is, a person may be able to read academic or even literary writing in an L2 and yet may have little experience in carrying on a conversation in the L2. Many international students arrive in the U.S. with well-developed CALP but lack BICS. This deficiency in oral/aural skills can potentially impede the students' ability to adapt psychologically to the new environment since, as a result of the difficulty they experience in speaking and understanding informal English, these students are likely to seek out and interact mainly with others from their own countries. Thus, lack of BICS proficiency removes a rich source of language input — social interaction.

Newcomers to an English-speaking country may also experience an overload of language input. Particularly if the L2 was learned formally in school, it is likely that the language input the students received was quite controlled. The learners may never have had to deal with any feature of the L2 they had not been formally exposed to. As a result, these learners may feel overwhelmed by the enormous sea of uncontrolled language they encounter in the L2 environment and the speed of oral interactions. Like culture shock, this "language shock" may cause learners to lose confidence in their ability to survive in the target culture. They may feel embarrassed or frustrated at not being able to say what they want in the L2 and fear appearing comical.

Individual characteristics of learners also have an important impact on how well an L2 is acquired. Ellis (1985) identifies the significant features of the individual's profile as age, language aptitude, cognitive style, personality, and motivation. The age at which learners began their formal study or informal exposure to the L2 appears linked to the ultimate level of proficiency attained in the

L2. Observations, studies, and just plain common sense show that the earlier learners are exposed to the L2 and the longer they stick with the language, the greater the level of achievement, at least of the skills the learners practice (Larsen-Freeman and Long, 1991). There does seem to be a "critical age" beyond which an L2 learner no longer develops the kind of competency which would make the learner's use of the L2 indistinguishable from that of a native speaker. For pronunciation, the age may be fairly young, perhaps as young as seven but usually closer to twelve or thirteen (Ellis, 1985; Krashen, 1981). Other age ceilings are not as clear. In other words, we do not really know if there is a critical age for the acquisition of a target grammar or whether age has an impact on vocabulary growth. Beyond the age of twelve or thirteen, however, factors other than merely the age of the learner seem to predominate in affecting the level of proficiency the learner can ultimately attain.

The role of aptitude for language learning is difficult to determine since aptitude itself is affected by other psychological, historical, and socio-cultural learner variables. The Modern Language Aptitude Test (Carroll and Sapon, 1958) purports to measure an individual's native ability to discriminate among unfamiliar sounds and to absorb grammatical patterns. Nevertheless, as with age, limitations resulting from a presumed lack of talent for languages are regularly exceeded thanks to other positive constellations of factors, such as motivation or length and intensity of exposure to the L2.

Cognitive style appears to be related to specific types of abilities in language acquisition. One of the most researched trait pairs is field dependency/independency. A field dependent cognitive style appears related to an ability to respond holistically to a learning environment, to see the forest rather than the individual trees. The strength of field independent individuals is in their ability to approach targets analytically, to see the trees in the forest. In an experiment on field dependency in which subjects were asked to repeat what they heard, field dependent individuals who made mistakes left out whole phrases. When field independent individuals made mistakes, they left out small details (Naiman et al., 1978). It is quite likely that these two learning styles interact with given learning environments in such a way that field dependent individuals learn better in one type of environment and field independent in another. In other words, a learner's ultimate achievement in an L2 may depend in part on whether the learner was lucky enough to be in a learning environment that matched his/her cognitive style.

Related to cognitive style are varieties in personalities. Field dependent people are more likely to be socially sensitive, to derive their self-image from others' view of them. Field independent people, on the other hand, are likely to have a more impersonal orientation and less social sensitivity, seeing themselves as more separate from their group. But it is not clear exactly what the impact of social sensitivity might be on language acquisition.

The question of how introverted or extroverted a learner is does appear to have an effect on language acquisition, although perhaps not the effect one would expect. Some suggest that introversion, not extroversion, is more positively correlated to language achievement because introverted people may be more empathetic, a personality factor related to successful language learning (Brown, 1980; Guiora, Brannon, and Dull, 1972). Extroversion seems to be related to the ability to generate interaction in the target language. High Input Generators (HIGs) appear to seek out opportunities to use the target language and to get others to use the target language with them. Their interactions are more frequent and longer than those of Low Input Generators and therefore presumably aid in at least the speed of language acquisition (Seliger, 1983). Finally, success in language achievement appears to be linked to ego permeability, that is, to the ability and/or willingness of an individual to take on a different personality or to let go of one's usual ego-defense mechanisms (Brown, 1980; Guiora et al., 1972). Ego-permeability seems to be the result of a combination of high self-esteem, willingness to take risks, and ability to empathize with others.[1]

All the factors mentioned so far—age, aptitude, cognitive style, and personality—remain more or less out of the control of the individual learner. But probably the most powerful factor in determining a learner's ultimate language achievement, one which is much more under a learner's control, is motivation. Motivation's power may come simply from the fact that the more motivated the learner is, the more likely the learner is to spend time interacting with the target language and the more proficient the learner will become. However, the role of motivation is complicated by serious socio-affective issues such as the status of the L1 relative to the L2, the attitudes of the speakers of the L1 toward the speakers of the L2 and vice versa, and the extent to which the L2 is imposed on the learner. High motivation is a tremendous facilitator of language acquisition, but high motivation develops as a result of a complex web of personal, social, economic, historical, and political factors. (See Chapter 4, "Characteristics of ESL Students," for further discussion of motivation.)

ESL students will appear in the writing classroom in every combination of personality, cognitive style, motivation, and level of proficiency in spoken English. These combinations will not necessarily be visible to writing teachers but will impede or facilitate ESL students' performance and progress in writing classes.

L2 Acquisition Models

If the analogy holds between acquisition of a foreign language and acquisition of that special variety of language use which is writing, writing teachers may find helpful a closer view of what might be going on as L2 learners progress toward fluency in English. Many partial theories of second language acquisition exist, nearly 150 by one count (Larsen-Freeman and Long, 1991)! In this chapter, I will cover in some detail the Monitor Model of second language acquisition and then touch on several others briefly, hoping to draw out their implications for writing.

Krashen's Monitor Model

The best known, most debated, and most fully elaborated model of L2 acquisition is Krashen's Monitor Model (1982). The model has a great deal of intuitive appeal and perhaps for this reason descriptions of the model have found their way into the professional journals devoted to L1 writing (Winterowd, 1983; Bartholomae, 1980).

The development of the Monitor Model seems to have grown in response to a notion of biological determinism which holds that developing native-like proficiency in a second language is possible only up to a certain age and that, after that age, a series of physical changes occur in the brain which interfere with or prevent the acquisition process. In adults, language function is located in the left half of the brain, while the right half governs holistic, gestalt perceptions. We know this because when adults experience damage to the left part of the brain, they often lose language function forever. When children experience damage to the same part of the brain, however, language function is not lost. In childhood, apparently, both the left and the right halves of the brain participate in language function, and if the left half is damaged, the right half can assume the responsibility for language processes. According to the critical age hypothesis, the critical age, when the brain lateralizes functions to the left and the right halves, is puberty (Lenneberg, 1967; Penfield and Roberts, 1959). Lenneberg noted in addition that it is also at about the age of puberty when people seem to lose the ability to become native speakers of an L2. He hypothesized that brain lateralization at puberty was the essential factor in preventing the development of native-speaker language ability. In other words, a learner who begins the study of or is exposed to an L2 after puberty would have no chance of ever developing the language abilities of a native speaker. Since lateralization is an inevitable stage in the normal development of the human brain, it was thought that success or failure in L2 acquisition might be biologically determined.

Krashen, however, cites evidence that, in fact, brain lateralization may be complete much earlier than puberty, closer to the age of five (1981, 73−76; 1973). If this is the case, then what is it that happens at puberty that seems to limit a learner's language learning potential? To answer this question, Krashen developed the five hypotheses of his Monitor Model of L2 acquisition.

In the first hypothesis, Krashen makes an important distinction between language acquisition and language learning. Acquisition is the unconscious absorption of language that takes place when children learn their L1. People acquire language by using real language for real communication. Learning, on the other hand, takes place during the process of consciously studying the rules of a language. Most students of an L2, especially adults, both acquire and learn the target language. But Krashen's insightful contribution to this distinction, which was already fairly well accepted but under other names (implicit/explicit knowledge of L2; analyzed/unanalyzed; automatic/controlled) lies in his insistence on the power of acquisition relative to learning. He makes the point that linguists claim to know and to be able to describe only a small portion of the rules of any natural language. Language teachers know only a small portion of what the linguists know. In their classes, language teachers teach only a small portion of what they know. Of that small portion taught, students learn an even smaller portion. In other words, it is impossible only to "learn" a language. Most of what we can do when we know another language is the result of acquisition.

Another extremely useful corollary to this distinction regards error correction. While error correction may have some use in helping a person learn, it seems to have little or no effect on the acquisition process. Krashen supports this position by referring to L1 acquisition. Studies show, for example, that parents rarely correct their young children's errors in language, and yet all normal children eventually learn to speak the same way as those in their language community do. That is, children do not maintain idiosyncratic versions of their L1 despite the errors they make as they are acquiring that language. Furthermore, when parents do sometimes correct children's grammatical errors, those corrections seem to have absolutely no effect, and the children continue to make those errors despite corrections until eventually the errors disappear on their own.

#2

These aspects of error correction are related to Krashen's second hypothesis, on the natural order of morpheme acquisition. Studies with children learning English as their first language show that the kinds of errors they make in the L1 are developmental and that the acquisition of the correct forms occurs in predictable sequence. But even more interesting are studies Krashen cites which examine the acquisition of morphemes by both children and adults *of different language backgrounds* learning English (Bailey, Madden, and Krashen, 1974; Dulay and Burt, 1974). These disparate groups also show a natural order for the acquisition of English morphemes — an order fairly similar to the order L1 learners go through. This work suggests that the acquisition order for both L1 and L2 is natural, fixed, and impervious to error correction.

#3

The third hypothesis, the monitor hypothesis, asserts that the rules that a learner does learn contribute very little to the learner's language ability; they can be used to monitor and clean up the learner's language output. In other words, rules learned through error correction and direct instruction in grammar may have a positive, albeit small, effect on language production. Unfortunately, the internal, mental language monitor which stores those rules can only be accessed under certain quite limited conditions. The learner must have time to access the rules in the monitor; the learner must be focused on the rules, as opposed to focusing on communicating a message; and the learner must know the rules. Very few communicative situations fulfill these conditions, and therefore, even if the learner could learn every rule of the L2 (impossible, of course, since no one even *knows* all the rules of any language), the usefulness of this knowledge is extremely limited. Fortunately, learners can acquire language without knowing rules.

#4

But how do learners acquire language? The fourth hypothesis maintains that learners acquire language through comprehensible language input at a level of difficulty just beyond their current level of acquisition. Children learn their L1 because parents want to communicate with them and use every means, every prop, every form of non-verbal communication they possibly can to get the message across. Krashen's claim is that the same is true for L2 learners. The input must be roughly tuned to the learners' current level of development. If the input is not comprehensible, the language becomes meaningless noise and no acquisition can take place.

But none of this addresses the problem of why older people do not seem to learn an L2 as well as children do. Krashen's last hypothesis states that affective factors play an important role in learning an L2. Krashen postulates the existence of an affective filter which prevents even the most comprehensible, meaningful, and communicative input from being taken in. If the affective filter is high, the learner will not receive the input. If the filter is low, the learner will be able to take in the input. This hypothesis is particularly important in relation to the age of the learner. At puberty, children become intensely self-conscious and psychologically vulnerable. At the same time in their cognitive development, Krashen suggests, they are passing through the stage Piaget called "formal operations" (1968). Just when they are becoming particularly self-conscious, they are also becoming increasingly able to think abstractly and to imagine other people's thoughts. What they imagine is that everyone is as focused on their behavior as they themselves are. To defend themselves against this threatening scrutiny, they raise all sorts of psychological barriers, including the hypothesized affective filter, which prevents L2 input from being taken in. It is this new strength of the affective filter (along with other environmental factors), not some physical change in the brain, that prevents individuals from excelling in an L2 after the age of puberty.

The message is a hopeful one. Affective variables can be controlled; L2 acquisition can take place in a setting which seeks to minimize fear, nervousness, and self-consciousness. (Note: Ironically, in the United States, many school children's first exposure to a second language takes place in eighth, ninth, or tenth grade — exactly the time when Krashen's work suggests these children are the most emotionally and psychologically vulnerable and *least* likely to be capable of taking the risks associated with language learning!)

I have described Krashen's insights at some length because they are particularly coherent and applicable to teaching writing. The distinction between acquiring and learning language appears pertinent to the accepted wisdom that good writers are good readers. It suggests that the ability to write well is acquired, in this special sense, through exposure to texts in a natural process of communication, not through the learning of rules of writing. A proficient writer who is not, or has not been, a prolific reader is a rarity. By extension, then, we might suggest that to learn to write English acceptably, learners require exposure to written texts in a natural process of communication rather than grammatical and rhetorical rules on writing in English. According to Krashen, the best way to learn to write is to get comprehensible input by reading material of personal interest at a level of difficulty roughly tuned to the reader's ability to understand (Krashen, 1984).

Krashen's theory questions the usefulness of focusing on errors during the acquisition of writing ability and suggests an answer to the question of why student writing errors, like the errors of children learning their first language, appear resistant to correction. Error correction, no matter how assiduously applied, simply has no effect on the *acquisition* process.

According to the Monitor Model, then, comprehensible input in the form of reading promotes acquisition of written language; learning rules of grammar, punctuation, and so forth is useful only to monitor, or edit, writing, not to create it; writers are stymied in their development by affective variables caused by their past failures and by criticism of their past attempts to write.

If Krashen's model seems plausible to help understand the problems of young writers, the tenets of the theory then seem doubly significant for young writers who are also non-native speakers of the language they are writing. Many of these students are convinced, often from their home country experience with language learning, that the way to learn an L2 is to study the rules of the language. It is not uncommon for ESL students to ask for a book which will teach them to write; I know of the case of one student who promised that if he were directed to the appropriate book, he would memorize one page each day in order to learn to write well in English. Studying a book on learning to write English is, of course, much less psychologically threatening than actually writing.

It is likely that the fear of failure, the pressure to succeed, and the nervousness caused by competing with native speakers in institutions of higher education cause a strengthening of the affective filter among many ESL students which gets in the way of their progress in English. The most insidious feature of the strong affective filter, however, is that it is hidden, hidden even from the learners themselves. There is no way to gauge how big or how strong the filter is, how much of what is offered as language input cannot be taken in by these students, whether for reasons of affect or of development (that is, they may not yet be ready to process that input).

But these students are individuals with varying learning styles. Some are what Krashen calls monitor underusers (1981), willing to blurt out whatever language forms come to mind without passing them through the grammatical censor of the monitor for correction. This may be especially true for ESL students whose training has been informal and oral. Others may be monitor overusers, so concerned about correctness that they are unable to develop any flow, any momentum in their writing. These are the students Raimes poignantly describes in her article "Anguish as a Second Language" (1984). When given a writing assignment, they immediately begin

to thumb through their tiny bilingual dictionaries, painfully search-
ing out each exact word.

Furthermore, although these ESL students are functioning in an
English language environment, it is quite possible that much of the
input they are getting is not comprehensible. The input may come
too fast and with too little repetition. Sometimes the input will be
incorrectly interpreted: a student of mine was mortified by a marginal
note on his paper commenting that it was a shame he did not have
more time to work on that paper. He understood the comment to
mean that he should be ashamed, not the intention at all.

Misunderstandings are also likely when the input is not grounded
in shared cultural experience which would allow the non-natives
to guess at meanings. One class of ESL students was completely
stumped by a text's description of one professor's attempts in the
1960s to get away from the traditional classroom structure by holding
class in his darkened living room. (Nowadays, this description
might stump native speakers too!) Certainly none of the words in
the reading were difficult to understand, but the interpretation of
the meaning of this professor's actions was only possible accompanied by an understanding of the cultural setting, an understanding which the students could not have had.

In addition, if the acquisition of language features progresses in
a more or less predetermined order, it is possible that no amount of
instruction (or correction) will allow ESL students to use certain
features of English correctly until they have eventually acquired
them. Errors in such late-acquired, troublesome features of English
as prepositions and the article system may simply have to be tolerated
until the students' exposure to English — the amount of comprehensible input they have taken in — is sufficient for them to internalize
correctly the way these features of English function.

Schumann's Acculturation/Pidginization Hypothesis

Other models of L2 acquisition focus on different aspects of L2
acquisition and also provide insights into the task ESL students
face. Schumann's acculturation/pidginization hypothesis (1978)
emphasizes the socio-cultural factors which influence acquisition.
Acquisition depends on the degree of acculturation or adaptation to
the target culture; this in turn depends on the degree of the learner's
social and psychological distance from the target culture. A good
learning situation in terms of social variables would include the
following (Schumann, 1978):

- Neither the target culture nor the native culture is dominant.

- Both groups expect members of the native culture to acculturate, that is, to adapt to the life style of the target culture while retaining their own culture.
- The members of the target culture and the native culture expect to intermingle socially.
- The L2 group is neither large nor cohesive.
- Both groups have positive attitudes toward each other.

It is easy to see how international ESL students might be much luckier in having these conditions met than immigrant ESL students, or other linguistic and cultural minorities in this country. A bad learning situation might come about as the result of a great deal of real or perceived social distance between the target and the native culture and also as the result of negative psychological conditions such as culture shock or language shock, in which the L2 learners experience doubt about their ability to understand or be understood in the target language. It is quite common to hear stories of ESL students who muster all their courage to ask a question in class and are unable to make themselves understood after several repetitions. The embarrassment caused by such incidents, along with the suspicion that the professor is perhaps refusing to understand, may have the effect of stifling any further attempts to participate in that social setting.

Schumann refers to Smith's (1972) three functions of language, which are also developmental stages: the communicative stage, in which the learner is concerned merely to communicate and receive messages; the integrative stage, in which the learner uses the L2 to mark the learner as a member of the L2 group; and the expressive stage, in which the learner uses the language to express virtuousity in the language often through creative writing. Under conditions of great social distance (which would reduce the amount of input available) or psychological distance (which would reduce the willingness or ability of the learner to turn input into intake), the learners' language will fossilize at the communicative stage, in which the learner will be able to use the language to get what he/she wants from the target culture but will develop limited capacity for full self-expression. This suggests, for example, that learners may be limited in their ability to use writing as a tool for learning. Writing remains alien, preventing these learners from making the powerful connections between thought and writing that permit reflection and learning.

Schumann's model illuminates the notion of writing students as initiates into various academic discourse communities. When the academy appears too distant, too cold, and too unwelcoming, both ESL and native writing students may resist the kind of acculturation or initiation into the academic discourse community which is expected of them in their writing classes.

Andersen's Nativization Model

Andersen's nativization model (1983) is an extension of Schumann's work. Andersen suggests that in less developed stages of acculturation, learners use their own internalized perception of what the L2 looks like to process new language input. But instead of accepting the reality of the L2 as an external norm, these learners nativize or assimilate the new input into their idiosyncratic version of the L2. In other words, in a bad learning situation, if learners are confronted with language input that does not conform to their internalized sense of the L2, they deform the input, forcing it to fit their picture of the language. Under good learning conditions, learners de-nativize, or accommodate their own internalized model of the L2 to conform to the new input. For writers, once again we have evidence that error correction may be pointless. If the writers are unconsciously forcing input to fit into their own scheme of the target language instead of reshaping their scheme to accommodate the input, corrective feedback on their writing will have little effect. In this model only an alteration of the social and psychological environment for language learning or for writing could potentially alter the learners' language intake processes.

Cognitive Theory

Cognitive Theory also addresses the question of what learners do with L2 input. Lightbown (1985) notes that L2 acquisition does not appear to progress linearly but rather is characterized by backsliding on linguistic forms which had seemed mastered already. She suggests that this backsliding may come as a result of a learning overload. As learners encounter new L2 forms and attempt to fit them into their internalized grammar of the target language, this work load causes errors to appear in theretofore stable L2 forms. The apparent backsliding may be the result of a restructuring of the learners' internal L2 grammar based on or forced by the encounter with new L2 forms that do not fit the learners' grammar. McLaughlin (1987) postulates that in an attempt to hold down the cognitive work load, learners simplify, overgeneralize, regularize irregular forms, and reduce language redundancy. When called upon to produce language, these learners once again employ strategies to reduce the work load formally by avoiding certain language structures which they are unsure of and by avoiding entire speech acts or functions (as in the case of students who no longer ask questions in class). Only as some forms become automatic do learners have time to take in new language input and re-analyze their internalized grammar in light of the new input. In terms of the writing classroom, this notion of cognitive overload and backsliding suggests that ESL students, coping with language learning as well as with learning to write, may in fact be making progress toward these goals even when surface evidence of improvement is not visible.

Interesting research evidence indirectly supports the cognitive overload hypothesis, suggesting that turning attention to one cognitively demanding task necessarily diverts energy from other cognitive tasks. In one experiment (Hatch, Polin, and Part, 1970), students were asked to delete the e's from a text. Better readers, those who attend to meaning rather than form, did worse on this task than unskilled readers. This suggests that perhaps unskilled readers attend excessively to form and are unable to attend to meaning because their cognitive capacity is already overloaded (McLeod and McLaughlin, 1986). Other studies (Rossman, 1981, cited in McLaughlin, 1987; Sachs, 1967) have attempted to determine where subjects turn their attention in a linguistic task. Attending primarily to meaning in a message, native speakers were able to detect alterations of the meaning but remembered changes in syntax less well. But non-native speakers remembered changes in syntax better than changes in meaning, suggesting that their processing of language forms was not automatic. The need to process the syntax of the message precluded attention to the meaning. For writers who must still focus a great deal on form, little cognitive energy remains for attention to meaning.

Neuro-functional Theories

Neuro-functional theories of second language acquisition provide yet another possible explanation for why formal language practice has so little effect on overall language ability improvement (Seliger, 1983; Lamandella, 1979; Selinker and Lamandella, 1978). Seliger suggests that the right hemisphere of the brain stores formulaic, unanalyzed language routines and patterns before the patterns are analyzed for manipulation and creative use by the left hemisphere. Learners may use these forms in the right hemisphere but only in whole chunks. Unless the chunks are analyzed by the left hemisphere, that is, somehow made a part of the learners' internalized grammar, learners cannot use these memorized patterns in creative, spontaneous language production. Such an understanding of these neurological processes might explain why grammar practice and memorization of language forms seem only minimally useful in writing contexts where language must be used actively to express personal meaning. These forms, stored as unanalyzed chunks, may remain inaccessible to the writer for active, creative manipulation.

Conclusion

All of these explanations of the L2 acquisition process describe learners in the same way, as individuals continuously in the process of actively attempting to analyze the L2 and sometimes, for a variety of reasons, unable to do so. All of these explanations help us to see why after ten years of studying English in classrooms abroad, ESL students still may have trouble writing effectively in English and why students who can recite grammar rules, as many ESL students do quite well, are not always able to use those rules in producing language. They should also help us to understand the difficulties inherent in learning an L2 and to accept that, like a foreign accent in speech, flaws in producing written forms can only be overcome by the most determined, assiduous learner, and even then perhaps only if the learner began English study before a hypothetical critical age. These L2 acquisition models also make it clear that L2 acquisition, like L1 acquisition, appears quite unrelated to intelligence and instead is tied more closely to an intricate network of social, psychological, and motivational factors.

SECTION II

THE STUDENTS

Chapter Three

English as a Second Language and Basic Writers

With the distinctive burden of learning to write and learning English at the same time, ESL students have needs which set them apart from mainstream English-speaking students. Unfortunately, when financial and personnel resources are not available to do otherwise, ESL students are sometimes lumped together with other students requiring special attention, particularly with basic or developmental writers, but sometimes even with hearing impaired students, often in classes considered remedial. A more principled argument for combining these groups has been that the difficulties these writers face and the strategies that may help overcome their writing problems are very similar (Roy, 1984). The difficulties are, in fact, at least superficially similar; some of the same strategies *can* be used, beginning with treating these students with respect; and under appropriate circumstances, basic, ESL, and SESD (Standard English as a Second Dialect[1]) writers can flourish in a mixed class. But it is important for teachers and administrators who propose these combinations to be sensitive to the potential conflicts created by mixing these students.

First, if ESL and SESD writers are taught in the same class, the class is almost certain to be a basic writing class taught by a non-ESL teacher accustomed to the needs of SESD writers but most likely untrained to deal with ESL students. It is important to keep in mind that while similarities between ESL and SESD students seem to exist, many are only superficial; furthermore, the strategies that work with SESD students cannot simply be assumed to work with ESL students.

27

Second, the fact that an ESL student is not proficient in English says nothing about whether or not the student can write. Many ESL students are graduate students with highly developed writing skills; and even ESL undergraduates may be as experienced and proficient in writing in their L1 as their native English-speaking counterparts in regular writing classes.[2] On the other hand, ESL students may be inexpert in English *and also* inexpert in writing. For these students alone, it may make sense to place them into basic writing classes.

Third, teachers and administrators need to keep in mind the role of affect in the language/writing class. If the notion of an affective filter has any psychological reality at all, successfully teaching ESL and SESD students in the same class requires careful maneuvering to avoid offending both groups and thereby reducing their chances for progress. SESD students may resent being in a class with "foreigners." Reminded daily and in many ways of their economic and/or social distance from the mainstream, they may regard their placement into a class with non-native speakers as insulting, yet another instance of their own marginalization. ESL students, on the other hand, may initially regard SESD students as educationally or intellectually inferior. After all, they reason, these students are native speakers of English, they have presumably spent all their lives in English-speaking schools; so why haven't they been able to learn to write? The ESL population is no more enlightened or free of prejudgments than anyone else. The classroom teacher may find it necessary to work continuously and systematically against the prejudices of both these groups if the class is to succeed.

On the other hand, the progress of these different groups may depend on factors beyond the control of the classroom teacher, but certainly worth being aware of, such as 1) linguistic complications, 2) personal history with Standard Written English (SWE), 3) cultural history, and 4) emotional factors surrounding the effort to change dialects or languages.

Linguistic Difficulties

Attempting to approach second language learning and teaching logically and systematically, linguists developed the tools of contrastive analysis and error analysis. Contrastive analysis compares two languages and notes the areas of difference. Error analysis, on the other hand, determines the difficulty of features of an L2 by cataloging the actual errors that learners make. Contrastive analysis assumes that the most difficult features of an L2 to learn are those that differ the most from the L1. However, we now know from error analysis studies that this is, in fact, not necessarily the case and that it is often the features of L2 which are close to but not identical with L1 which are the most difficult to master (Schachter, 1974).

Since dialects of English are closer to SWE than are other languages, it may be linguistically more difficult to change dialects than to change languages. SESD students may not even be aware of differences between their dialect and SWE because the dialects have similar elements and are more or less mutually understandable. (See Bruder and Hayden, 1973, for further discussion of these issues.) If it is true that for strictly linguistic reasons some features of second dialects are more difficult to master than some features of second languages, ESL students would seem to have some kind of linguistic advantage over SESD students and may actually be able to make faster progress than SESD students toward familiarity with standard written forms.

A second potential advantage which ESL students may have over SESD students relates to register, or degree of language formality. Most ESL textbooks, even those that aim to be conversational, teach the more formal registers of English, those closest to SWE, rather than strictly spoken forms. ESL students may be acquainted with spoken forms but are, in fact, more likely to use too high a register in speech than too low a register in writing. For example, an ESL student might say *moreover* more readily than saying *besides*. Since in L1 development we learn informal spoken registers first and then the more formal written registers, ESL students may give the false impression that they have already mastered everyday spoken forms, have moved beyond them, and speak with studied formal elegance. With SESD students the opposite may be true; that is, SESD students may employ too informal a register in their writing, falsely appearing uneducated. Thus, the ESL students' familiarity with formal registers may appear to work to their advantage.

A corresponding disadvantage, however, is that ESL students may not be familiar with everyday spoken forms. A common mistake in dealing with ESL students is attempting to communicate by simplifying language from more formal (which native speakers assume to be more difficult) to more informal (which *for native speakers* is easier to understand). But informal vocabulary may actually be more difficult for ESL students to understand. An international student might talk about *extinguishing* a cigarette but may not quite have mastered *put out* (one of English's notorious two-word or phrasal verbs) and might confuse *to put out* with *to put off* or *to put on* or *to put over*.

It is conceivable that ESL students' familiarity with more formal registers of English gives them another advantage. Formal registers are characterized, among other things, by a greater degree of linguistic redundancy. According to register studies (see Joos's 1961 descriptions of frozen, formal, consultative, informal, and intimate registers of English), intimate and informal registers exhibit a greater lack of redundancy and lack of background information than do more formal registers. In using the informal register, the speaker assumes shared background information with the listener; in more formal registers, information has to be made explicit, including linguistic information like matching subject and verb number or tense with adverbial time elements (since + present perfect, for example). Thus, regardless of whether they are indeed able to supply that redundancy, ESL students, more accustomed to formal registers, may be more sensitive than SESD students to the need for making background and linguistic information explicit.

Personal Histories with Writing

Like most language learners, ESL students are unlikely to have had much experience with writing in English beyond doing grammar exercises, writing answers to questions, and producing occasional paragraphs as a test of grammatical mastery more than as a means of consolidating knowledge or expressing opinion.

SESD students, on the other hand, have probably had plenty of experiences with writing, probably most of them bad. And since success in many academic disciplines is measured to some degree by success in written expression, students in developmental or basic writing classes have likely had twelve years of failure in writing and perhaps in other subjects as well. They may carry with them the baggage of low self-esteem and low expectations for themselves. They complain to their writing tutors, "They tried to teach me this in high school; I guess I'm just too dense to learn" (Havens, 1989). In addition, these students are likely to suffer from writing apprehension; they may fear taking the risk of exposing themselves in writing. Since, as Mina Shaughnessy (1977) has pointed out, SESD students have not identified the reasons for their failure in writing, they may consider their dialects "bad" English. And in fact, in the very separation of SESD students into basic writing classes, an inescapable value judgment is made about these students' dialects, and by extension about them.

People's self-perception and sense of identity are very much bound up in language and in their use of their native language. Anyone who has ever studied a foreign language has probably noticed how much more potent and resonant swear words, or love words, are in the native language. By the same token, a great deal is at stake in the suggestion that SESD students use bad English. That criticism goes to the core of their identities; it implies they are not literate in a society that equates illiteracy with stupidity. For ESL students there is much less ego-involvement than for SESD students. ESL students expect to make a lot of errors; they want and expect corrections. Errors and corrections are perceived much less as signs of their own failure than they may be for SESD students. Thus, because of their personal histories with writing, ESL students are less likely to become deeply discouraged and pessimistic about their chances of success in the L2.

SESD students are likely to come from economic ghettos and to have suffered exclusion from mainstream culture their entire lives. This is not at all true of ESL students, who, even if they are not wealthy, are less likely to have suffered racial, socio-economic, or cultural isolation at home, let alone here, and so have not had to build the emotional and psychological defenses that SESD students may need.

Furthermore, again unlike developmental students, many L2 writers come to English already highly literate, only not in English. After all, many international students are graduate students. Most have been successful students and writers. As far as their writing in English is concerned, they see themselves as merely temporarily deficient in a particular skill, like a respected novelist who is learning to use a word processor. ESL students generally have high self-esteem. They sometimes even claim to be great writers in their own languages. Even in those cases when they are not good writers in their own languages, they rarely feel mortified at this admission. ESL students may have been weak in English at home but that weakness did not mean success or failure in school and certainly did not stigmatize them any more than being weak in French in high school would stigmatize native English-speaking students in the United States.

ESL students also are much more likely to have the respect of their English and content-area teachers despite problems with writing in English since they are, after all, writing in an L2; just by coming from another country they have had experiences that privilege them, that may even make them the envy of their teachers. It is less likely that teachers would envy or perhaps even be interested in the experiences of SESD students.

Both groups of students may be forced to combat preconceived ideas about themselves, but, ironically, faculty's negative reaction to "bad" writing may fall more heavily on SESD students than on ESL students. While these faculty may forgive non-native English speakers for making mistakes in English, they may be less forgiving with second dialect students, perhaps because they assume that what second dialect students need to learn should already have been learned. Studies of faculty reactions to ESL errors (Santos, 1988; Vann, Meyer, and Lorenz, 1984) suggest that faculty members find highly irritating and unacceptable certain errors resembling those native speakers are likely to make, like double negatives, subject/verb agreement errors, and, in some cases, spelling and punctuation errors.[3] Presumably, these faculty see the irritating errors as editing errors, those that could be avoided with careful re-reading (Kroll, 1991). The fact that the errors are there implies that the writers have been careless or lazy or have not taken the writing assignment seriously. Worse yet, these errors among native speakers may be considered what used to be called "illiteracies," suggesting that students who make them are illiterate.

If faculty is more forgiving of ESL students' errors, the role SWE will play in ESL students' future lives may also result in far less motivation to master written English. Educational goals and purposes for learning to write may be very different for second language and second dialect students. While second dialect students can be expected to use a wide variety of writing skills in their personal and professional lives after college, it is quite possible that ESL students may never have to use written English again once they leave the United States or will have to use only a very limited range of writing skills. Furthermore, if ESL students leave the U.S. university unable to write English well, this failing is far less stigmatizing for them in their home countries than such a failing would be for SESD students. Writing well may be crucial for SESD students' future success; writing English well may have negligible effect on the professional futures of ESL students.

Cultural History

In their struggle to write academically acceptable English, ESL students probably have another ally in the role that writing plays in their native cultures. In many cultures, the written word has an extremely elevated status. Whatever is written is, somehow, the truth. The privileged who know how to write are the most respected people in the culture. In some Asian cultures, knowing how to write *means* being educated, since learning to write entails learning thousands of ideograms with direct links to cultural and literary history (Matalene, 1985). In Europe, Africa, and Latin America, writers become national leaders: Havel in Czechoslovakia, Senghor in Senegal, Vargas Llosa in Chile, Cardenal in Nicaragua, Fuentes in Mexico; even school children know and respect the work of nationally renowned authors. Semitic cultures too have an extremely elevated opinion of writing and the writer. Rabbis were the learned, the keepers of knowledge because they could write. Islam reveres the written word as a form of privileged communication with God, and respects any religion that has a sacred book; writing is holy. ESL students from these cultures come to English with a respect not only for the written word but also for their own cultural history.

SESD students, on the other hand, in addition to possibly considering their own language a corruption of "real" English, often have been taught no awareness of their own linguistic traditions, no respect for their own dialects, no understanding of the linguistic equality of dialects. African-American students, for example, are unlikely to have been taught about the impact of West African languages on English. How many are aware of the creolization theory which suggests that Black English is not an altered form of English but rather a Creole which became decreolized to be more similar to English (Bruder and Hayden, 1973)? The history of these dialects has in effect been suppressed. Thus, it is not surprising that SESD students are unlikely to be proud of their own dialects. They may even despise and deny their own seemingly a-historical speech. An experimental basic writing class with a group of African-American SESD students used contrastive analysis to make the students aware of differences between standard English and Black English; the students reacted extremely negatively to seeing Black English dialectal forms written on the board for comparison with SWE, characterizing the examples of Black English as ignorant and rural and insisting that no one they knew spoke that way (Bruder and Hayden, 1973). Some Appalachian dialect speakers are equally disparaging of their own language, thinking of it as "country," "hillbilly," and ignorant (Caudill, 1963).

Whether or not SESD students despise their own dialects, they face another problem in their effort to acquire SWE. SESD students may have an enormous and sometimes unconscious resistance to displacing their own English forms with those of the dominant class, something that is not usually a problem for ESL students. People's use of language as a means of identifying themselves with a desired group is extremely difficult to work against. Sindlinger (1981) reports a case study of a young Hispanic-American woman who wanted to improve her accent in English. While she made considerable progress in the language laboratory, in the real world she did not use her new Anglo accent. Sindlinger suggests that her desire to identify with her Hispanic peers and not to be identified with the dominant culture precluded imitation of the Anglo accent in the real world despite her consciously expressed desire to "lose her accent." It is possible that SESD writers are working at similar cross-purposes with themselves.

Thus, SESD students have a great deal to struggle against, both linguistically and psychologically, in their study of SWE, but they also have certain advantages as native speakers of English which ESL students do not have.

Strategies

David Bartholomae (1980) makes the excellent point that basic writers are not thirteenth graders writing like seventh graders; rather they have an idiosyncratic version of SWE. They are not learning the language; they are learning to use a particular variety of the language in a particular way.

ESL students are not thirteenth graders writing like seventh graders either; they too have an idiosyncratic version of SWE. But they *are* learning the language, both the spoken and written variety. ESL writers are likely to violate much more basic categories of English — for example, placement of adjectives: a day beautiful. They are more likely than native speakers to misunderstand classroom interactions and may understand only a fraction of classroom management talk. SESD students can easily do interesting and relaxing assignments which include going to the movies, watching TV, or listening to the radio; for ESL students these assignments will be much more like work.

Native English-speaking basic writers lack options in their use of SWE (Bartholomae, 1980), but this is much more true for non-natives, who nevertheless keenly sense that options exist. In other words, ESL writers may feel quite acutely that their thoughts are far more varied and subtle than what they can express in English and that they *would* be able to express these thoughts well in their own languages. (See Chapter 6 for further discussion of ESL students' perceptions about writing in English.)

Thus, SESD and ESL students have very different strategies available to them in writing. SESD students may, for example, be able to substitute spoken dialectal words and forms for SWE and stand a fair chance of at least being understood. But for ESL students every word may be a struggle. In writing they usually cannot fall back on spoken forms the way native speakers can since they are unlikely to know the spoken forms either. If ESL students write "many informations" instead of "much information," no appeal to which phrase "sounds right" will help, as it might for SESD students. To ESL students neither may sound better or worse.

Several published studies (Rose, 1989; Butler, 1980; Bartholomae, 1980) have mentioned an editing strategy available to SESD students: reading their papers out loud. As they read, SESD students are often able to correct written errors automatically. Using sophisticated top-down processing strategies in reading, they see the words they meant to write instead of the words they did write. They use the meaning they intended to express to predict the words they are reading. This strategy is much less available to ESL students, who often seem barely to understand what they are reading out loud even though it is their own writing. Research evidence (Nattinger, 1978) shows that SESD students have very little trouble compared to non-native speakers in using context or the linguistic environment to predict the words to fill in the blank spaces in cloze passages. Even advanced ESL students are much more likely to use bottom-up reading strategies, trying to guess the meaning of what they are reading from the graphemes on the page, rather than top-down strategies, using meaning to anticipate the words on the page; as a result, they are much less able to correct errors that appear there.

Another strategy which may be much less successful with ESL students than with SESD students and which is recommended in one-on-one conferencing is a kind of counseling strategy in which the teacher repeats back to writers what the teacher assumes they meant. In this way, both teacher and students can determine whether the message came across. This technique may work less well for ESL students for several reasons. Even if the teacher's summary misstates their ideas, ESL students may agree with it either out of politeness or because they did not quite understand it and are reluctant to question the teacher. It is also possible they will agree with the summary because they may feel that the teacher's summary is better than their own statement of what they are trying to express. They may be tempted to say that the teacher's words are, in fact, the ones they meant to say themselves. In other words, they may alter what they wanted to say to fit what they think the teacher wanted them to say. It is possible that SESD students, too, are intimidated enough to accept any interpretation the teacher may give even if it does not match their intention, but it is less likely than with ESL students, just as it is less likely that the SESD students would not understand the teacher's summary.

Further lightening the burden for SESD students, and to some extent even for hearing impaired students, are the many shared cultural and linguistic assumptions and experiences which their teachers can tap to help these students progress. ESL students share far fewer of those assumptions or experiences with their teachers. International and visa students have comparatively little time to acculturate to the United States and to U.S. universities. Even after years here, they may be excluded from understanding countless cultural references. If there were ever any doubt about the uselessness of such compendiums as the *The Dictionary of Cultural Literacy* (Hirsch et al., 1988) for native students, it is clear that for ESL students no amount of memorization of items in a listing could compensate for the failure of these cultural references to resonate with the experience of those raised in another culture.

Hearing Impaired Students

Some post-secondary institutions apparently practice the reprehensible policy of recruiting special students, like ESL students or hearing impaired students, and, after collecting admissions fees, not providing these students with the special facilities they require to succeed. A recent positive trend in the TESOL organization[4] has been to examine which insights and techniques from the ESL profession might be useful in teaching SWE to the hearing impaired. However, frustrated at the problems hearing impaired students have in regular freshman English classes and taking advantage of the fact that SWE is clearly a second language to hearing impaired students, some university administrations have simply provided a translator and dropped these students into ESL classes, expecting the ESL teacher to figure out how to deal with these students' special needs. It is extremely rare to find ESL, basic writing, or regular freshman composition teachers with any qualifications whatsoever for teaching the deaf.

The issues are complicated, and a sense of their complexity may help writing teachers to resist irresponsible practices at universities which fail to address the special needs of hearing impaired students and which simply group all students with special needs into ESL or basic writing classes. The community of teachers of the deaf have long debated the value of Signed English (based on the structure of English) versus American Sign Language (a language with a structure of its own unrelated to English and more suited to signing). The relationship between signed languages and SWE, or any spoken language, remains unclear. The fact that signed languages are visual and simultaneous, not linear, has unresolved implications for teaching the hearing impaired. Furthermore, few teachers of the deaf are deaf themselves and many signers are not particularly good at it, not "native speakers" of signing (Strong, 1988). In fact, the language input that deaf children get may be totally inconsistent, coming from hearing parents who do not sign well but use Signed English or from peers who sign a creolized combination of Signed

English and American Sign Language. It is a tribute to the amazing flexibility of the human mind that, despite such confusing input, these children still learn to communicate.

The language history of these students is complex and requires much more attention than it has received. What seems clear, however, is that the ESL classroom, or the basic writing class, should not be used as a dumping ground for hearing impaired or any other special category of students by universities that do not know what else to do with them. The students deserve more respect than that.

Conclusion

Although ESL and SESD students (and hearing impaired students, for that matter) are different from each other, come from different educational and life experiences, and have differing needs to some extent, all of this is not to say they cannot benefit from working together in the same writing classroom. In fact, many argue that ESL and SESD students derive specific benefits from finding themselves in the unusual position of being able to offer expert help to a classmate. What ESL students are good at, SESD students may need more help with, and vice versa. Nelson (1991), for example, describes a successful writing tutorial program in which basic writers and ESL writers worked together with a tutor in small, four-to-six-member groups and were able to support each other and to improve their writing.[5]

The point is to rely on principled reasons to combine these groups of students, not merely reasons of convenience or finance, to hire appropriately trained and experienced instructors for these classes, to recognize the differing needs and abilities of these groups of students, and to capitalize on them in classrooms where these students may find themselves together. Teachers in such writing classrooms and administrators who place students there need to develop a supportive atmosphere in which students do not perceive studying together as punishment or as degrading to their perceptions of themselves and their roles in the educational environment. Teachers and administrators also need to make careful assessments in planning the curriculum of these courses. Over and over again in the literature on basic writers, researchers and teachers point out that these students *do not* need additional work with minuscule details of writing conventions or the print code (Rose, 1989; Bartholomae, 1980; Shaunessy, 1977). In many cases this is also the case with ESL students. In some cases, however, ESL students do need additional experience with grammar, rhetorical conventions, and the print code, as well as with reading and writing. ESL students have not had a lifetime of exposure to English texts.

Benesch (1991) has argued that tracking or dividing and subdividing groups of students based on ever more refined differences among them is pointless; differences will always exist even in the most subdivided of categories of people. Mixed groups of students can learn from each other in good writing classrooms. Although we need to remain aware that superficially similar problems in writing may result from radically different causes and to adjust our courses to address the real causes of these problems, the question of root causes of linguistic problems may nevertheless become irrelevant under certain conditions. In one mixed class Benesch describes, the writing class is linked to a content course which focuses on the oppression of various minority groups by Europeans in North America in the 19th century. The individual students in the mixed class have been able to draw together on the basis of their common history and current status as minority groups in the United States. In this instance, the special content focus of the writing class, as opposed to a linguistic focus, has the effect of uniting these students around their historical similarity rather than dividing them on the basis of their linguistic differences. As many argue (Benesch, 1991; Rose, 1989), a focus on content in a writing course produces positive linguistic, discursive, and attitudinal changes in both ESL and SESD students.

In any case, decisions about tracking ESL, SESD, or basic writers clearly can only be made locally, taking into account the types of courses offered, the pedagogy of those courses, and the nature of the students taught.

Chapter Four

Characteristics of ESL Students
Varieties, Expectations, Experiences

If ESL students are unlike basic writers, they are also unlike each other. Actually, they differ so much that it is not an exaggeration to say that sometimes the only similarity they share is that they are not native speakers of English. ESL students are graduate students and undergraduates; forty-five years old and eighteen years old; highly educated doctors, lawyers, teachers in their home countries and naive, inexperienced teenagers; newly arrived immigrants, graduates of U.S. high schools; poor writers in English but good writers in their L1, poor writers in their L1, or illiterate in their L1; those hoping to remain in the United States, those eager to get back home; those extremely critical of life in the United States or U.S. foreign policy and those wholly in support of anything the United States does. They are also diverse in their expectations of life in the United States, their financial situations, their levels of academic achievement, their willingness to integrate into their temporary new society. Although much of the information in this chapter and in Chapter 5 is based on personal experience (mine and that of colleagues) and is therefore necessarily anecdotal and somewhat fragmentary, I nevertheless feel that becoming aware of some of the personal characteristics of ESL students will help teachers better understand them.

Although most international students come to the United States to continue their educations, many other different reasons for coming underlie this similarity. Some plan simply to get degrees which will help them get good jobs in their home countries. Others use a quest for education as a means of getting permission to leave their countries temporarily, but in fact intend to leave forever, sometimes entering into marriages once here for the sole purpose of being permitted to stay, sometimes disappearing from official view and hoping not to be detected. Still others, usually more privileged, study in the United States for a year or two simply to expand their horizons, much as U.S. students spend a junior year in Europe. Finally, some students come to the United States less interested in studying than in escaping wars or internal strife in their home countries. Their attitudes toward their experiences here will be greatly colored by their reasons for being here.

Socio-political factors influence not only students' reasons for coming here but also their attitudes and experiences once they arrive. They may come from countries which have had hostile relations with the United States or from countries which have been adversely affected by U.S. foreign policy, that is, countries whose citizens are generally unsympathetic to the political role the United States plays in their country or in the world. The students themselves may be attempting to overcome revulsion at U.S. policies. The question of what kind of political relationship the students' home country has or has had with the United States may be crucial to the students' ability to function or even live in safety in this country, as evidenced by the attacks on Iranian students in the United States during the "Hostage Crisis" in 1979−1980 and on Arabs during the 1991 Gulf War. Both Iranian and Iraqi students at times felt impelled to pretend to be some other nationality in order to escape violence resulting from political disputes between the United States and their governments.

Another question to consider is how U.S. citizens react to other nationalities. While French or British students can in general expect to be well received, African students are often quite fearful of the effect American racism will have on them personally. Asian students may escape institutional discrimination only to experience personal resentment directed against them as a result of their reputations for being excellent, hard-working students — whether or not they are. Haitian students were pariahs when Haiti was being blamed for the AIDS crisis. Finally, while a single Laotian or Russian student may be the object of friendly curiosity on the part of the educational and broader community, these same communities may consider droves of students from the same part of the world threatening and react negatively to them.

Depending at least in part on their origins, ESL students may have widely divergent expectations of the United States and stereotypical views of U.S. citizens. They may experience the United

States as a veritable Sodom and Gomorrah or, on the other hand, as utterly provincial. Several years ago a group of eighteen-year-old Libyan students came to study at my university. None of these young men had ever lived outside his village. Most had never even spent a night away from their families. Coming to the United States to study caused a great deal of emotional strain, as these young people tried to come to terms with cross-cultural experiences they were unequipped to handle. One hot summer day I suggested to one of these Libyan students that he try to cool off by studying at the University's Aquatic Center, the Olympic-sized swimming pool where undergraduates gather to read or relax. Nervously, he rejected that idea, quickly explaining that there were naked girls there and he couldn't even walk by the place, let alone study there.

On the other hand, other students come to the United States from the capital cities of the world; many are very sophisticated. Europeans, for example, have expressed astonishment that the university will not permit them to invite their dates to spend the night with them in their dorm rooms. They find such rules quite provincial, even insulting.

Some expectations are confirmed; others die. The point is that the expectations themselves can create fear and insecurity among international students. How can these students react emotionally, for example, to the very wide-spread perception that Americans do not make good friends, that they are self-centered, individualistic, too busy making money or taking care of their own business to be able to show any real warmth in human relations? There is a complex relationship between the expectations of these students and the kinds of experiences they actually have.

In terms of finances, some ESL students are on small government scholarships or are supported by families who can ill afford to send a child abroad but who have put all their hopes for the future into their child's education. These students live on a meager allowance under a great deal of pressure to finish their expensive educations abroad as quickly as possible. They look for the cheapest housing available — and find it, to the shame of the landlords collecting rent on the damp, dirty, windowless basement apartments, often in the most run-down, dangerous parts of town.

Other students are also supported privately but come from wealthy families. One Saudi Arabian student of mine wore only clothing advertised in *GQ* magazine and had a taxi take him back and forth to class every day, at $15 a ride.

It is often assumed that ESL students are uniformly the brightest students from their countries. After all, they are studying in a foreign language. But the range of abilities and academic achievement among ESL students is quite wide. Many international students are, in fact, among the most intelligent and accomplished individuals from their countries. But many others are quite average and come from countries with either very few universities or with excellent and extremely competitive universities. Their academic records may not have been strong enough to admit them to universities at home, but they may have been admissible to less demanding U.S. institutions. Attending even a mediocre institution abroad may confer a certain amount of prestige. In the case of Japan, for example, young students work extremely hard throughout their elementary and secondary school years to gain admission to a few prestigious Japanese institutions of higher education. Admission to these schools virtually guarantees the best jobs after graduation no matter how well or badly the students actually do once admitted. Since admission to lesser institutions in Japan does not carry much prestige, students ineligible for admission to the most prestigious schools may feel that continuing their schooling abroad is the best option available to them.

ESL and Permanent-Resident Students

Perhaps the most important distinction to make among ESL students, however, is between permanent-resident or immigrant students and international students. Permanent residents are most likely to want to integrate into this culture; they are likely to want to be viewed like any other U.S. student, even when it comes to English. One Vietnamese student, for example, insisted on taking the regular freshman composition course with native speakers. She had graduated from an American high school and did not want to be placed in courses for "foreigners," as she said. Unfortunately, she unsuccessfully repeated the regular composition course three times before agreeing to take the special composition course for ESL students (where, incidentally, she flourished).

Permanent-resident ESL students are likely to know all the icons of American teen culture but may be suffering from anomie, that is, confusion about which culture they actually belong to, that of their families or that of their new peers in the United States. International or visa students usually do not at all mind associating with other internationals and often feel more comfortable with these students than with Americans since other internationals are experiencing similar adjustments and problems. The internationals typically are not interested in being taken for Americans.

Immigrant or permanent-resident students and international students are also likely to differ in their ability to communicate in English. Many immigrant or permanent-resident students are quite proficient speakers of English but may be much less skilled in writing; they may or may not be literate in their native languages. On the other hand, most international students are highly literate in their own languages and often much better in reading and writing English than in comprehending or speaking it, particularly when they first arrive in an English-speaking country. Furthermore, international students from countries like India or Nigeria, countries which use English as a business language or as one of the country's official languages, may speak a dialect of English which English speakers in the United States may find quite difficult to understand, particularly since these students are so accustomed to speaking English and are likely to speak very fluently and rapidly.

Learner Motivations

Whether the student is a permanent resident or an international will probably affect the kind of motivation the student will bring to learning English. Gardner and Lambert (1972) distinguish between instrumental and integrative motivations. Instrumental motivation refers to the learner's desire to learn the new language in order to accomplish some other goal, for example, to study or conduct business in that language. Integrative motivation, however, refers to the learner's desire to integrate into that language's discourse community.

If the L2 is a foreign language, as, for example, French is here, then integrative motivation appears to correlate better with language acquisition. Many of us are familiar with the college student who spends her junior year abroad in France and returns looking and behaving more French than the French. Her motivation was clearly integrative and that motivation probably helps to account for the tremendous progress in language which these students make in the target country. However, if the L2 is truly a second language in a country (as English is in the Philippines) and is used to accomplish specific goals, then instrumental motivation is more strongly associated with success in language acquisition (Gardner and Lambert, 1972). In either case, it is not clear whether these motivations affect second language acquisition or whether success in language acquisition inspires greater motivation.

Culture Shock

ESL students come with both types of motivations. Some ESL students are not the least bit interested in becoming "Americanized," while others immediately take on all the trappings of U.S. college culture. Both motivations can be powerful, but they hold different implications for weathering culture shock. Students with an instrumental motivation may be less invested emotionally in their experience with the new culture and language and may initially suffer less from the inevitable ups and downs of cultural adjustment. Integrative motivation, on the other hand, may cause students to build firmer support systems and help them better tolerate long-term separation from home.

As they adapt to a new culture, nearly all non-native students experience culture shock to a greater or lesser extent. The transition from one culture to another follows fairly predictable phases (Lewis and Jungman, 1986). Most people experience an initial euphoria and feel intensely interested in everything about the new culture; they are struck with the monumentality of their own undertaking, of the very fact of being in the new country. As they begin to interact with the new culture, however, they experience both defeats and victories, causing alternating frustration and self-confidence. Succeeding or failing at tasks as simple as purchasing a stamp at the post office can create emotions completely out of proportion to the task itself. As they become more familiar with the new environment, they take more risks and experience more bruises. The more familiar they feel with the new culture, the higher the expectation of success and the more painful the bruises that continue to occur.

It is usually at this point, after the initial euphoria and after a series of emotionally bruising incidents, that culture shock sets in. People experiencing culture shock suffer from depression; they become passive, pessimistic, lethargic, irritable (Lewis and Jungman, 1986; Larsen and Smalley, 1972). They may lock themselves in the safety of their rooms to escape the dreaded new culture and new language and seek out others from their own country partly to combat loneliness and homesickness but also to complain bitterly about all the faults of the new culture and its people. They also experience feelings of failure (Others have done this, why can't I?) and of self-pity. During this time these students will be less flexible, inventive, and spontaneous than normal. Since their usual coping mechanisms do not work, they may revert to child-like dependence on others and become exhausted from trying to accomplish even routine activities (Scarcella, 1990).

Fortunately, as inevitable as culture shock is for most people, recovery is normally also inevitable. Increased interaction with the new culture eventually results in a more normal distribution of likes and dislikes of the new culture and people and in the development of the self-confidence needed to continue to interact successfully within the new culture.

Oddly enough, the phases of cultural adjustment appear to accommodate themselves to the length of time anticipated in the target culture. Thus, the sojourner will not be able to escape phases of the adjustment merely because the stay in another country is short. Rather, all the phases are experienced, but each one is condensed (Lewis and Jungman, 1986).

The intensity of these phases of cultural adjustment for any individual depends on a variety of personal and cultural factors. While any human being may suffer from culture shock, some may be particularly vulnerable. It is worth noting that many international students come from cultures in which families are much closer than typical American families, much more dependent on each other for support. These people make tremendous personal sacrifices and may endure intense emotional pain at their separation from their families. For economic or political reasons these students may be unable to see family members for years. A not untypical example is a graduate student of mine from the People's Republic of China, who left her infant son in his grandmother's care six years ago and has not seen him during this entire time.

As if these problems were not enough, most people experience reverse culture shock upon their return home, going through similar phases of adjustment. These adjustments, however, may be even more painful since not everyone knows to expect them and since they bring on intense feelings of anomie, of uncertainty about which culture one belongs to. Returning students may find their families not as fascinated with hearing about their experiences abroad as the students are with recounting them; their families may prefer to recount local events whose importance has dimmed for the student returning from abroad. A Tunisian student writes in his journal that on his first visit home after a year in the United States, he was constantly annoyed by his friends' references to events he had missed during that year. But his saddest moment came when he realized that his family had abandoned their traditional spot for drinking afternoon tea — under their peach tree. Clinging to that bit of stability and tradition, he writes that he refused to abandon the past and continued to sit under that tree by himself until his family finally gave in and joined him.

Conclusion

If we are to be of any help to international students, it is important to be aware of these phases of cultural adjustment. As we deal with students in our classrooms or offices, we cannot at a glance know whether they are in the emotionally devastating but entirely predictable phase of cultural adaptation that is culture shock. In fact, it may be the success or failure of the very encounter students have with us that sends them into the abyss of culture shock or pops them out into the adaptation phase. Simply recognizing that a student's irritability or lethargy is part of a phase of cultural adaptation may help us to react more helpfully to the student's emotional state.

Chapter Five

Classroom Expectations and Behaviors

Most of the time ESL students are not traumatized, just surprised, surprised at the receptions they get here and surprised at some of the customs and behaviors they encounter in U.S. classrooms. International students are often hurt and insulted by American ignorance of, and disinterest in, their home countries. American undergraduates are notorious for such geographical gaffs as placing Canada on a map of Texas; Malaysia may as well be in outer space. One international student was upset to learn that his American classmate had never heard of Thailand. African students are asked if people live in houses in Africa. French students have been asked if they have refrigerators in France.

All this is disheartening coming from college students, but international students have more serious problems to face. Although many faculty members are interested in international students and friendly toward them, in disciplines and perhaps parts of the country where there are many non-natives enrolled as students, these students sometimes encounter hostility from their teachers. Certain professors build a reputation of disliking international students in their classes and of automatically giving them lower grades. How prevalent such a practice is probably cannot be determined, but certainly students believe it happens.

Students have reported other behavior on the part of some professors which is, at the very least, unbelievably insensitive, perhaps racist. One student's content-area teacher took his paper and tore it into pieces, telling the student to learn English before turning in a paper. Another student reports:

Right at the beginning the professor said that I could not pass the course. He said, "As long as you have a Japanese mind, you can not pass 111." When he said this I thought I could not survive sometimes. I have had a Japanese mind for 30 years how can I change it? I felt so depressed. The teacher said that he had had a Korean student who had taken 111 three times in order to pass. He compared me to the Korean saying that it would take me at least that long. I felt like he thought all Asians were the same — Korean Japanese there's no difference. This felt like racial discrimination to me. (Newstetter et al., 1989)

International students fare as badly in the community. A student from Hong Kong claims that he is regularly overcharged for purchases in his conservative Southeastern community and that residual, confused resentments from the war in Vietnam cause locals to automatically take him for Vietnamese and discriminate against him. (His hilarious and ingenious solution to this problem was to announce that he was not foreign; he was just from California, a location probably as distant and exotic to many of these local residents as any place in Southeast Asia!)

Classroom Expectations

Different national groups and different individuals bring different expectations to the classroom, but many students express surprise at the same aspects of post-secondary classroom culture in the United States. Many of the surprises are pleasant. Some international students come from educational systems in which famous scholars and researchers deliver lectures to several hundred students at once, never getting to know any of them personally, or even speaking to them individually. These students are pleased to find that many of their professors here are approachable, informal, and friendly, that they set up office hours when students are welcome to discuss concerns privately. Some students are also thrilled with the flexibility of the U.S. university system and with the diversity of completely unexpected classes available, like typing or various physical education classes.

On the other hand, ESL students often remark on the apparent lack of respect for teachers here, shown in the casual clothes, sandals, even shorts, that their native classmates wear to class or in the eating and drinking that may go on in some classes. The whole teaching environment is disturbingly casual to some students. Teachers sit on the front desk while lecturing, students interrupt lectures to question or dispute what the teacher has said, teachers sometimes say they do not know the answer to a question. Any of these behaviors may jolt the expectations of non-native students.

Even something as simple as what students and teachers call each other can create confusion. Some international students feel uncomfortable calling teachers by names and prefer to use only titles, addressing their instructors simply as "Doctor" without using a name or using a first name, as in "Professor Ken," or simply using "Teacher." Students from the People's Republic of China tend to address their professors by their last names only: "Good morning, Johnson." By the same token, of course, they may expect to be addressed by their family names only and feel uncomfortable being addressed by their given names, an intimacy reserved for only a few very close family members. Even husbands and wives may refer to each other by their family names. Many of the international names are difficult for linguistically provincial Americans to pronounce, and students often resort to taking on English names while they are here. One Jordanian student writes that his name has been spelled and pronounced in so many different ways that he now responds to anything even vaguely resembling Najib: Jeeb, Nick, Nancy.

Many international university students also have a hard time adjusting to what they see as being treated like high school students. They are amazed to find teachers demanding daily attendance, assigning homework, and policing the class by testing periodically to make sure they have done the homework. These students may come from a system in which students may choose to take advantage of class lectures or not, as long as they pass a comprehensive, end-of-the-year exam. Quite a different attitude toward student responsibilities from our own!

In some countries, students may take pre-departure classes or U.S. culture classes which may cover some of the areas of difference between educational practices at home and abroad and thereby help students prepare for their experiences. But these courses cannot cover every encounter the students may have. One international student, for example, took a multiple choice test here for the first time. Having had no previous experience with this form of testing, the student assumed that multiple choice meant choosing more than one answer per item (Stapleton, 1990). Other students come from educational systems in which competing theories are presented only in order to explain the correct theory. The students are confused when they realize that their professor here assumes none of the theories is entirely correct (Krasnick, 1990). It is important to keep in mind that in addition to learning subject matter in a class, ESL students are also often learning a whole new approach to learning itself.

Classroom Behaviors

It should not come as a surprise to us, then, that these students will not always do what we expect in our classes. International students have stood up when the teacher entered the room; others have insisted on erasing the blackboard after class for the teacher. A student of mine, misconstruing the idea of office hours, complained that he had come by my office, hoping to find me by chance for a conference at 5:00 P.M. Saturday afternoon. That student said he waited for me for an hour!

Some students have a difficult time with the style of class participation they observe. While U.S. teachers may consider class participation an important sign that the students are paying attention, some ESL students will never participate unless specifically called on. They may be especially reluctant to volunteer answers to questions since they may feel that by doing so they are humiliating their classmates who cannot answer the question. A Japanese proverb says something like, "The nail that sticks up gets hammered down." Compare that to our own, "The squeaky wheel gets the oil."

ESL students may also react badly to teacher requests for opinions, especially opinions in conflict with those expressed by the teacher. Such requests may be viewed as evidence of teacher incompetence (Levine, 1983, cited in Scarcella, 1990, 94), and many ESL students are trained specifically *not* to hold opinions differing from those of their teachers. By the same token, ESL students may expect teachers to know the answers to any question they may have; these students may become embarrassed and lose confidence in teachers who honestly state that they do not know an answer but will find out. In one case, an Iranian student whose chemistry teacher had made such a statement dropped the class, explaining that he did not see the point in trying to learn from someone who did not know. In Iran, he explained, a professor would sooner fabricate an answer than admit to not knowing.

Many other types of assumptions come into conflict in culturally mixed classes. In an article on attitudes toward time, Levine (1985) describes a problem familiar to ESL teachers — ESL students' flexible attitude toward deadlines. This professor describes his first day teaching at a university in Brazil. Fearing he will be late for his first class, he asks several people the correct time and gets different answers from everyone he asks, answers differing by twenty minutes! Some of the casual strollers he asks are, he later realizes, students in the very class he was in such a rush to get to on time. Once in class, he notices students coming in fifteen minutes, thirty minutes, even an hour late, and none of them act embarrassed or chagrined or apologetic. And when the class period is over, none of them get up to leave, willing instead to stay on another fifteen, or thirty, minutes or whatever it takes to get their business done. People in many other countries are simply not driven by the clock in the way people in the United States are. As a result, even though ESL students usually know of the U.S. reputation for, they might say, fanatic devotion to punctuality, these students sometimes just cannot bring themselves to conform to class starting times and paper deadline dates. Their priorities are such that they may be unable to refuse to help a friend in need even if their term papers are due tomorrow. In one 8:00 A.M. class of mine, students from Greece, Zaire, and Palestine arrived in class every single day from five to fifteen minutes late; on the other hand, a group of students from the People's Republic of China arrived every single day from five to fifteen minutes early!

Traditional gender roles may also create problems for ESL students. For some of these students, their experience in the United States will be the first time they have been in a mixed-sex classroom. This alone may be intimidating for them. But in addition, in some parts of the world, women are expected not to speak in the presence of males at all, clearly posing a special problem of classroom participation for these students. Even if women students do not have this additional burden placed on them, they, and males from these cultures, may feel awkward working in groups together and, if given the choice, may choose to work only in groups of the same sex.

It is also the case that some of these students, particularly the males, may never have had a female professor and may need some time to adjust themselves to that new experience. ESL professionals also cite instances in which gender prejudices make male ESL students unable to take female authority figures, including teachers, as seriously as they would males. But general respect for authority and for teachers in particular apparently overrides these prejudices for the most part. These problems occur with very few students and far less often in English-speaking countries than in the students' home countries.

Language

Language obviously creates misunderstandings. Even though ESL students may be paying careful attention to what is going on, they may actually understand only a portion of what they hear. New ESL teachers consistently register surprise at their own overestimation of how much their students understand of classroom management talk. Numbers in particular may be difficult, for example, the page numbers of reading assignments. These students may need to have directions repeated even when they claim to have understood. In fact, for students from some cultures where it seems to be taken for granted that all credit for students' learning belongs to the teacher, it may be utterly useless to ask if they understand. For cultural and linguistic reasons, they may always claim to understand even when they don't, either hesitant to bring further attention to themselves by their failure to understand or reluctant to imply that the teacher has not made a point clearly enough.

Sometimes the confusion arises because, for some cultural groups, nodding the head, which indicates agreement or at least understanding to English speakers, may merely indicate that the listener is continuing to listen, while perhaps not understanding the content of what is being said at all (Scarcella, 1990). For some Arabs, blinking the eyes indicates agreement, a gesture unlikely even to be noticed by uninformed native English speakers, and for some Indians, the gesture used is tilting the head to the side in a movement that resembles the English gesture indicating doubt! (This gesture looks like the one which might be accompanied in English by "Oh well" and a shrug.)

Some languages are spoken with a great deal more intonation or emphasis than is usual for English. If students from those language backgrounds have not learned to imitate English oral delivery style well, they may come off sounding more vehement or emotional than they intend. Other students, many Asians, for example, may seem excruciatingly shy because of the longer pauses they customarily take before answering a question put to them. An English speaker may perceive a Vietnamese speaker as not participating in a conversation because the Vietnamese speaker takes so long to reply; the Vietnamese speaker, however, may perceive a series of friendly questions as a barrage implying impatience and not permitting appropriately reflective answers (Robinson, 1985, cited in Scarcella, 1990, 103).

Another aspect of the problems caused by language, even for students who are fairly proficient in English, may occur when a student tries to make a point. The rules for turn-taking vary among languages. A person speaking English is expected to heed verbal and kinetic cues indicating that the listener is now ready to speak, cues like taking a breath or making a sound toward the end of the speaker's sentence. Non-native students may inappropriately interrupt a speaker because turn-taking is handled differently in those students' cultures and they may not yet know the correct signals to send in this culture. In some cultures, interrupting a speaker may not be rude; it may be a sign of listener attentiveness intended to show the listener's involvement in the interaction. But it is also entirely possible that while the speaker is speaking, the non-native student is rehearsing what she or he planned to say and simply has to begin speaking before the planned sentence slips away.

Language-based confusion also arises unexpectedly and in ways impossible to guard against. One example is the Asian student mentioned in Chapter 2 who interpreted the comment "It's a shame you didn't have more time to work on this paper" to mean "You should be ashamed of this paper."

The confusion may also be on the teacher's part. Oral English proficiency, for example, including accents, can be extremely misleading. ESL students who have learned English in an environment which precluded much contact with spoken English may speak with accents very difficult to understand but may write quite well. Conversely, particularly with immigrant students, the students' oral English may sound quite native-like but their written English may be a problem. They may be quite proficient at BICS (see Chapter 2) but may have had little experience with CALP, the language of the academy. In either case, accents cannot be equated one way or the other with proficiency.

Grades and Exams

One very important area in which cultural assumptions may differ and cause friction is evaluation. Some of these students are under tremendous pressure to get good grades either because their financial support depends on maintaining a certain average or because their pride or family honor requires excellent performance. In addition, in many countries around the world, exam results are extremely important, determining much more absolutely than we may be used to here a student's admission to certain types of educational tracks or to certain prestigious schools and ultimately to a desirable job and life style. Even exams taken at age five or six can set children on the road to a comfortable, financially secure future or to a lifetime of factory work. Students from these countries take exams extremely seriously.

Further complicating the exam issue is the fact that it is taken for granted in some countries that friends and relatives have the right to call upon each other for any help they need, and that that call must be answered. Some students feel as much obliged to share exam answers or research papers as they would to share their notes of that day's class or to share their book with a classmate. (See Kuehn, Stanwyck, and Holland, 1990, for a discussion of ESL students' attitudes towards cheating.) Knowledge may be thought of more as communal, less as individual property. The moral obligation to share, to cooperate, to help a friend or relative makes far more pressing demands on some of these students than the obligation our culture may wish to impose of individual work and competition. In other words, what we call cheating is not particularly uncommon or shocking for some of these students. It simply does not carry the onus it does here.

In places where personal relationships have more weight than they do here and adherence to impersonal rules has less weight, bureaucrats and others in authority often have a great deal more flexibility to act than they might here. As a result, arguing, persuading, and bargaining for a better deal is a part of human interaction. That includes, of course, bargaining with teachers for better grades. In situations where students are pleading for higher grades, the justification is nearly always the same: not that the student actually did better, not that the teacher's judgment was wrong, not that the student does not deserve the lower grade, but that the student *needs* a higher grade and that it is in the teacher's power to *help.* When the teacher refuses to help, the student may go away hurt and confused, personally wounded at the teacher's indifference to the student's plight. These are very painful experiences both for the student and for the teacher, but particularly for non-ESL teachers who may not understand that the student (and the teacher as well, obviously) is operating according to another set of culturally determined rules about personal interactions. Non-ESL teachers may well come to resent international students for putting them in such tense, embarrassing situations and making them feel guilty about sticking to their decisions.

In these awful confrontations, it is also not unheard of for students to exhibit more emotion than most U.S. post-secondary teachers are accustomed to dealing with. Men in other cultures, for example, are permitted to cry under a much wider range of circumstances than is permitted here. Unrestrained sobbing is sometimes a student's response to the sadness of failure or defeat.

Body Language and Socio-linguistic Snags

Other conflicting cultural styles may be less dramatic but also disconcerting. Latin American and Arab students may sit or stand too close during conferences; Vietnamese students may feel uncomfortable with a friendly pat on the shoulder; Japanese students may not look at the teacher when addressed. During a discussion of

body language, I asked a class of international stud.
they noticed that people use eye contact differently i.
States from the way it is used in their home counti
students strongly felt that this was the case. When asked t\
a man from El Salvador complained that Americans refus
him in the eye, as if they were lying, insincere, or hiding sc
and a woman from Japan claimed that Americans made _r feel
uneasy because they seemed to insist on staring at her when they
spoke, right in the eye instead of somewhere at the base of the
throat, as she was accustomed to doing!

Cultural differences can cause other complications which are
not strictly linguistic. One of the experiences Americans abroad
often complain about is suffering the injustice of having someone
butt in line and be served out of order while those in line continue
to wait. But in many other cultures, people assume that those who
are waiting in line are in no particular hurry and don't mind not
being waited on next. If they did mind, they would be aggressively
demanding attention by pushing to the front of the line and stating
their desire. Students from these places, then, may feel quite comfortable crowding the teacher after class and demanding attention
while other students patiently await their turns.

Other embarrassing moments may occur as a result of socio-
linguistic differences among cultures. One of these areas concerns
the tacit rules which govern topics of conversation. Teachers may
feel intruded upon by questions which are completely normal in
the students' cultures: In Asia: Are you married? How old are you?
In the Arab world: How much did that cost? Do you have sons? In
Eastern Europe: How much money do you make? How much do
you weigh? (Wolfson, 1989) The reaction to such questions may be
outrage unless we realize that the question of what is appropriate to
talk about is a part of the linguistic system of a language that must
be learned just as verb tenses must be learned. Just as the questions
above may strike us as inappropriate, others take offense at different
questions. Muslim students, for example, are offended by questions
like "Why don't you drink?" or "Have you ever kissed your boy-
friend?" (Wolfson, 1989) Unfortunately, socio-linguistic rules are
not visible as rules, are taken for granted, and are assumed to be
universal. As a result, while grammatical errors may be ignored,
socio-linguistic errors brand the non-native as rude and offensive.

Notions of modesty about achievements also differ among cultures. Writing teachers may find it difficult, for example, to learn
whether a writing assignment went well for given students. When
asked how well they did on an assignment, Asian students invariably
say they did not do a good job, that they are not good students,

while Arab students seem to always reply that their paper is very good, that everything went exceedingly well.

ESL students may actually behave in ways that strike us as unusual, unexpected, or even inappropriate, but difficulties may also arise as we simply misinterpret what appears to be ordinary, recognizable behavior. The Japanese, for example, have an aversion for direct disagreement and instead of saying no to a suggestion may hedge, preferring to indicate vaguely that the decision must be postponed or further studied (Christopher, 1982, cited in Wolfson, 1989, 20). As a result, an English speaker may not recognize that the Japanese speaker has said no and may assume that the Japanese speaker really is still debating the issue. The Japanese apparently do not even like to say the word "no"; when asked whether she liked Yoko Ono, one Japanese student replied, "Yes, I hate her."

Finally, the offices of ESL teachers are often crowded with Chinese paper cuttings, Korean fans, Latin American *mulas*, and pieces of Arabic brass. Non-ESL colleagues of mine with ESL students in their classes have sometimes expressed concern that these gifts look like bribes and have wondered whether or not to accept them from their students. But this type of gift-giving is an accepted part of many cultures, and ESL students often give their teachers small gifts as tokens of respect and gratitude with no baser intentions in mind at all.

Students may misinterpret us as well or feel confused about how to interpret our signals correctly. While they may be happy to learn, for example, that professors have office hours, they may feel unsure about whether or not they are actually invited to take advantage of them. Students may be confused if the decision of whether or not to come by the office during office hours is left up to them and may conclude that an off-hand invitation to come by if they have problems, an invitation which does not *urge* or order the student to come by, is not sincere.

Conclusion

It takes some time for international students to determine exactly what their relationship with a professor is. Many of them come from cultures, such as China, in which teachers are highly respected but also are expected to behave more like mentors, to involve themselves in the students' lives, to know about them as people, and to guide them closely in moral, personal, or educational decisions. These students may then be disappointed to find this is not usually the case here.

Clearly, there is a great deal of room for both misunderstanding and resentment during confrontations involving different cultural styles. For the most part, it is the international students, outnumbered as they are, who will have to make the greater part of the adjustment to accommodate U.S. classroom expectations. But an awareness of some of these students' expectations on the part of their U.S. instructors can certainly make the adjustment easier for all. Anticipating some of the behaviors of culturally mixed groups can help us be more tolerant of them and perhaps at the same time less hesitant about pointing out, if necessary, the inappropriateness of some of these behaviors within the culture of the U.S. college classroom.

COMPONENTS OF ESL WRITING

Chapter Six

Writing Behaviors

Much of the confusion caused by the differences between international students' expectations and the reality of our classroom customs and behaviors is hidden from us. Teachers usually come into most direct contact with international students, however, in their writing.

Content of Papers: Sophistication

Since the range of ESL students' backgrounds is so broad, they are often a far more disparate group than students in typical writing classes, and their written work covers the gamut from amazing sophistication to similarly amazing naiveness. Because these students profit from experiencing and comparing at least two cultures, their understanding of the world often far exceeds that of their U.S. counterparts. These students, having left their countries, are likely to examine their culture, reflect on it, compare it to that of the United States. Such reflection becomes a great well of resources for writing, resources missing for all but a few of our native students.

Many of the international students who study in the United States come from wealthy families and, as a result, have profited from the privileges of wealth. They may have traveled extensively and have had routine contacts with people in positions of power and visibility in their home countries. Since many developing countries have relatively small middle and wealthy classes, professionals of all kinds are drawn from a small group of people. Thus, middle class students from Colombia, for example, have friends who are lawyers, doctors, famous artists and journalists, disc jockeys, singers, and political leaders.

Even international students who come to the United States on athletic scholarships are different from the usual athlete recruited by a state university. Most international athletic scholarships are for sports like golf, tennis, or swimming — the sports of upper classes who can afford the costs of country club memberships where these activities may be learned and practiced. These international athletes are likely to have had more worldly, broadening experiences to draw upon in their writing than the average college athlete.

In addition, many of these students know well that when they return home they will become government ministers or leaders of other types, sometimes by virtue of the very fact that they have studied in the United States. It is perhaps this consciousness of their future roles in their societies which engenders an occasional tendency toward speech-making in the writing of some of these students.

Regardless of whether or not international students are wealthy, they are nearly always very aware of their own cultural and historical heritage and can refer to it as readily as to the events of their own lives. I once wondered out loud to a blond Jordanian student why so many Jordanians are light haired and fair skinned. He retorted, "The Crusades!" These students also generally have more political sophistication than native students. Some have been through revolutions; some have seen their countries transformed dramatically in their lifetimes. They are often much closer to those kinds of changes than are young people in this country, who are so often politically naive or a-political altogether.

Many international students come from places where politics play a vital role in everyday conversations; their political commitments are firm and thoroughly argued through. For these students, politics is the most interesting and important subject in their lives. In a paper discussing cultural traditions in Jaffa, a student from Palestine devoted about the last fifth of the paper to an angry denunciation of Israeli occupation of Palestinian territory, a totally unrelated subject. Yet, his classmate from Yemen, writing a peer response to this paper, judged that section to be the best part of the paper.

This is not to imply that the global awareness of international students is so great. A student from Venezuela may be as unaware of or naive about events in Namibia or Cambodia as the most ostrich-like of native students but will know a great deal about Cuba, Nicaragua, and Panama. It may come as a surprise that a survey of undergraduate native and international students showed the international students not doing much better than the native students on general questions of geography, history, or science, but they did far better on subjects specifically affecting their own countries, including questions about the United States, than native students did (Leki and Wallace, 1988).

Finally, what international students write is often new for their teachers here and, as a result, seems sophisticated, innovative, and interesting. These students have a tremendous advantage over native students in this regard since their readers really may not be aware of much of what they write about, giving them excellent practice in accommodating the needs of an audience. If a student describes, for example, a traditional wedding ceremony in Vietnam and emphasizes aspects of the ceremony that are specific to Vietnam, she is bound to interest her non-Vietnamese readers. But as important a personal experience as a wedding may be, a native writer describing a wedding will have to work very hard to find an angle that will be of any interest whatsoever to most native readers. Native writers may need to work hard to find subjects to write on that their peers and/ or teachers do not already know everything about; international students have a wealth of such subjects. Exploring insights on the differences between high school and college life may be an important and personally expanding exercise for a young native student, but again to make such a subject worth the trouble to read is a struggle. Though international students may have no greater insight, they do have more unique material to work with; as a result, they routinely produce astonishing papers. A Japanese student fascinated his entire writing class with his description of how the Japanese use blood types to guess at personality traits and how young Japanese girls use these indices to select boyfriends. If he had been describing horoscope analyses of personalities to a class of natives, the paper would probably have been a bore. But what was commonplace in his home culture was a novelty for his readers; his task of engaging his readers was greatly simplified.

In another example, Chinese students' writing style often includes lyrical references to nature and novel (to English speakers, at least) metaphors. Such devices are relatively uncommon in the writing of young native speakers and, therefore, cause Chinese students' writing to stand out as particularly refined, though these devices, like the moral lesson included in so much Chinese writing, may simply reflect Chinese rhetorical preferences.

On the other hand, of course, experienced ESL writing teachers eventually grow as weary of reading about the Chinese Lunar New Year as freshman composition teachers do of papers discussing high school and college life. While a first encounter with even a straightforward description of the Chinese Lunar New Year may enchant a writing teacher, it probably bears keeping in mind that such a subject presents little challenge to the ESL student and, consequently, may not result in much growth for that student as a writer.

Naiveness

Although international undergraduates generally do have more novel experiences to draw upon for their writing than do most native students, the writing of ESL students may also seem particularly naive to a North American audience. For example, many ESL students have little information about or experience with social problems quite familiar to native students. Although they may be fascinated with divorce, drugs, or crime, they often have little firsthand acquaintance with these subjects. (They may, for example, never have known anyone who has been divorced.) As a result, there is a tendency among some ESL students to unreflectively repeat stereotypes of what they have heard about these subjects. Drinking, for example, leads straight down the path to drugs, crime, prostitution, and murder; so does divorce! Smoking among teenagers leads to drug use and hanging around with criminals. These students' papers on social problems sometimes read like the 1930s anti-marijuana movie *Reefer Madness.*

Partly because many of these students come from cultures in which families are very close-knit and partly because these students are away from home and perhaps homesick, enormous reverence for the family, for the mother and father particularly, turns up in their writing. But another factor which may result in a tone of pious reverence for parents may come from the view young people in other cultures may have of themselves and their role in life. In analyzing differences between the writing of Thai and American young people, Bickner and Peyasantiwong (1988) suggest that the Thai students' piety may come from their view of adults. Unlike American young people who see themselves at the pinnacle of their lives and somewhat self-centeredly see the world as revolving around themselves, Thai young people see the adult world as the center of life and are confidently awaiting their turn to step into those adult roles. This attitude may also explain why the writing of students from these cultures is so often preachy. In writing, these students take on the role usually reserved for adults of claiming the floor, in a sense. They may be practicing what they see as the adult right to hold forth, to expound wisdom. (Certainly, inexperienced native writers sometimes fall into preaching as well and perhaps for the same reasons.)

Similarly, partly because of the personal and financial sacrifices required by an overseas education and partly because of the traditional values of their cultures, many international students believe deeply in the value, importance, and prestige of a good education. This unquestioning devotion to studying and to education may find expression in devout clichés about the importance of learning English, even to the actual detriment of language improvement. Kessler, Heflin, and Fasano (1982) tell the story of two Vietnamese brothers learning English in California. The brother who made the most progress spent his time hanging around Americans, chatting and having fun with them. The other brother felt that such activity was a waste of time, time which needed to be spent on education. He spent his time alone in his room studying and in his writing constantly brought up the importance of studying, of getting an education, and of learning English, precisely what he was missing because of his very reverence for studying.

The sometimes overly dogmatic, assertive, and know-it-all tone of some of the writing of international students may also come from a respect for education. Those who write are the educated; those who are educated have the right to take an immodest professorial tone, often a tone chiding the rest of the world, for example, for not having solved such problems as pollution. A student from India writing on the injustice of *sati* (the traditional practice of wives immolating themselves on their dead husbands' funeral pyres) adopted the tone of an opposition politician on the campaign trail, berating the government in quite personal terms about their failure to stop such practices and calling on readers/listeners to throw the rascals out. Students who adopt this tone in their writing may be simply trying out the professorial persona they associate with the educated and powerful.

While William Perry's (1981) categories of cognitive development in young adults may be applicable across cultures and may therefore explain the firmness with which these students sometimes express opinions, it is also the case that the dogmatic self-assuredness expressed in some of the writing of these students has its roots in culturally based role assignments, with the educated retaining the right to take uncompromising positions and vehemently express strong opinions. That students from some cultures tend to express themselves in more authoritarian terms is suggested by research with Chinese and Australian students (Hu, Brown, and Brown, 1982, cited in McKay, 1989). Both groups were asked to write short answers to the following question: "Pretend that you have a brother who does not work hard at school. What would you say to persuade him to work hard?" The Chinese students took the position that their brothers had a duty to their country to work hard and framed their responses to the brothers in imperatives. The Australians never mentioned duty to country and framed their responses as tentative suggestions. It appears, then, that students from different cultures construe their rhetorical role differently.

The tone of authority that some ESL students adopt, however, may be misleading. Research (Prothro, 1955) has shown, for example, that what is taken to be exaggeration by one culture may be viewed by another as neutral; and what may be regarded as neutral by one culture may seem understated to another. Thus, ESL writing may appear overly emphatic (the writing of native speakers of Arabic, for example) or, on the other hand, overly demure (the writing of native speakers of Japanese).

Another factor influencing the degree of sophistication or naiveness North American readers may perceive in the writing of international students is caused by the transparency of each person's own ideology and culture. What seems obviously good, right, or moral in one's own culture can be challenged by contact with other cultures. International students, then, may be stunned to find themselves suddenly called upon to defend the givens of their native world when other students or teachers challenge practices they may take for granted. An Egyptian student of mine was very distressed at the disgust expressed by his friends when he mentioned that women in an Egyptian family typically eat together in the kitchen after serving the male family members in the dining room. His unsuccessful attempt to convince his friends that women are revered in Egypt confronted him with an altogether unfamiliar interpretation of a familiar practice. Other students' American friends express horror at the thought of cutting off the hands of a thief; or object to the idea of Islamic women wearing veils; or find it strange that people twenty, thirty years old and even older still live with their parents and take orders from them; or question why the birth of a baby girl should be sad and embarrassing to the mother. Non-native students suddenly find themselves having to defend what they may never have heard questioned before. In a literature class, the students were reading "Everything That Rises Must Converge," a Flannery O'Connor short story (1961, in Drabeck, Ellis, and Pfeil, 1982) in which a son is constantly irritated at what he considers his mother's embarrassing stupidity, and he continually criticizes her. In the discussion of this story, a young Indian man could not see why his classmates criticized the son's behavior; after all, he said, women *are* ignorant and it is, in fact, a son's duty to correct his mother. Such unexamined assumptions appear in the writing of these international students frequently but are all the more striking, of course, since they are often not the same unexamined assumptions we have.

The many stereotyped images of U.S. life also appear in the writing of these students. The most prevalent image is the violence of life in the United States. Many internationals see this country as the land of guns and gangsters. Students coming here are often quite frightened by our enormously high rates of crime and unconcerned acceptance of violence in the media. Many also see this country as a dangerous den of sin. They may accept as shocking fact the stereotype that American women are sexually forward and immodest, that homosexuality (the word is often pronounced in a hushed tone) is engaged in openly and tolerated by all, and that people with AIDS (it used to be herpes) are everywhere. Several years ago a seventeen-year-old Saudi student wrote of his uneasiness about coming to study in the United States. He was afraid to shake hands because he had heard that *most* people in the United States had herpes and that this disease could be spread by any physical contact. He also claimed that for some time after his arrival here he spoke to no young women because he was afraid that friendliness to an American woman would be taken as a request for sexual intimacy he did not desire!

Many ESL writing teachers claim they can guess fairly accurately the national origin of international student writers by recognizing certain characteristic features. They maintain that students from the People's Republic of China consistently say that we must work hard and progress; students from the Arab world say that things are good, or that they will become good, with a tone of resignation; Europeans complain. Temporarily suspended between two cultures, international students have a great source of experience to draw upon for their writing; at the same time, a great many unexamined assumptions and stereotypical images also find their way into this writing, all the more striking since they rarely correspond to our own assumptions and stereotypes.

Writing on Personal Subjects

While students who have gone through the U.S. educational system are accustomed to and for the most part comfortable with writing personal reactions to a reading, expressing opinions on topics which they know little about, voicing personal tastes, or recounting personal histories, these types of self-expression may be not only foreign to ESL students but may demand far more personal disclosure than they can tolerate and may therefore be sources of acute embarrassment for them. Thus, some ESL students are *least* comfortable writing what might be the easiest type of writing for American students, the personal essay. When required to write on such subjects as "My most embarrassing (or happy, exciting, sad, and so forth) moment," ESL students sometimes feel so uneasy using personal experiences or examples to support general statements that when forced to do so, they fabricate the experience rather than talk about themselves.[1]

Furthermore, there is the issue of what constitutes proof in a culture. In some cultures, personal experience counts; in others, personal experience is simply irrelevant to support a position. Instead students are required to quote famous writers to support their points.

Some cultures do not encourage the kind of self-orientation or insight-orientation of the personal discovery essay but instead encourage outward, group-oriented writing, for example, focusing on group or national achievement. As a result, some ESL students may not have much experience with or interest in written introspection of the kind we encourage native students to do. In a fascinating description of the kind of confusion created by encouraging students here to find their own voices, Fan Shen (1989) reveals exactly how difficult such a suggestion is for some ESL students. When told to be himself, he realized that he could not at the same time be himself and fulfill the teacher's assignment since being his real self would mean writing like a Chinese, in forms utterly alien to the U.S. college environment in which he found himself. He could not be himself at all. Instead, he had to develop an "American" self who was not him but who could fulfill the assignment in the way expected in this writing context.

If, as some have claimed, personal discovery writing is an artifact of ESL, freshman English, creative writing, and literature classes (Horowitz, 1986c), it should be no surprise that some new international students have had no previous experience with this form of writing.

However, this inexperience with writing from a base of personal beliefs is not the case for all the many different groups of international students that appear in English writing classes. An Iranian student of mine explained what a difficult time she was having defending positions she took in writing for her classes in the United States. In Iran this student had always been encouraged to express her opinion in her school-sponsored writing but had never been put under the obligation of defending a position she took, only of expressing it. She experienced frustration when she found that her professors in the United States demanded some sort of support for every stand she took in writing. It was not really clear to her even what constituted that support in this culture. Her innate sense told her that she had an opinion, that everyone has the right to an opinion, that opinion by its very nature is not open to challenge, and that all opinions carry equal weight by simple virtue of being held. Such a position, of course, recalls Belenky et al.'s (1986) description of women's cognitive development in the United States. However, the number of international students of both sexes and, more importantly, of all ages and apparent stages of cognitive development who express the same frustration this student felt argues in favor of a cultural rather than a strictly cognitive basis for this attitude toward expressing opinions in writing.

Issues in Topic Selection

Whatever may be the causes for disjunctures between ESL students' writing and U.S. expectations about writing, it is clear that teachers who wish to help ESL students must be particularly careful about the kinds of writing assignments they make. Many teachers no longer choose topics for students to write on, but those that do need to choose sensitively and judiciously. Unlike the Iranian student mentioned above and many native students, some ESL students may feel quite uncomfortable expressing opinions on subjects they do not know much about. In other cases, certain topics are inappropriate. Japanese students, for example, may find it unseemly to be asked to discuss religion in any form (McKay, 1989); Islamic students, on the other hand, seem to relish writing about Islam.

It may also be difficult for teachers to know what kind of writing topic is motivating for international students. Writing about gender-related issues such as dating may be quite interesting to native students and absolutely unsuitable for ESL students from certain countries. Topic selection is particularly difficult for newly arrived international students, who have not had enough experience with the United States to be able to use life here as a frame of reference and whose teachers cannot know what they have had experience with. Obviously, topics which are clearly culture bound will not work. But even topics which international students can write on may bring surprises. McKay (1989) recounts that when asked to write a narrative that involved taking a bus, Chinese students in China who had never been to the United States took the idea of riding a bus for granted, while international students studying in the United States and writing on the same topic felt the need to include in their narrative an explanation of why they were taking a bus at all rather than driving a car. Thus, while both groups of students were able to write the narrative requested, clearly the reality of their lives gave these students quite different perceptions of what had to be covered in the essay and what did not.

Another important consideration in making writing assignments for ESL students is related to the question of how information is stored in the brain. In his study of the link between information storage and language, Friedlander (1990) assumed that experiences which took place in the students' home country were stored in the brain in the students' native language, and that experiences and information obtained strictly in the United States — for example, registering for U.S. university classes — would be stored in English. He reasoned that if the language of storage and the language of writing matched — that is, if the students wrote about their native holidays in their native language and about registration at a U.S. university in English — the resulting texts would be rated higher than texts written under mismatched conditions — that is, writing about native holidays in English and about registration at a U.S. university in their native language. The results of his study do, in fact, show that students tend to write better if they are writing in the same language in which their memories are stored. This finding has significant implications for teachers making writing assignments for international students. If the students are asked to write in English on topics which are stored in their memories in their native language, they will, *even if they are very familiar with the topic*, be at a disadvantage both in retrieving the appropriate information and in formulating their ideas on paper. Thus, topics which may be extremely fruitful for native speakers — childhood experiences, personal history — may prove to increase rather than lighten the linguistic and memory-retrieval burden of ESL students.

Another consideration in making writing assignments for international students is related to writing prompts or the description of what the writing assignment is. Prompts are sometimes misinterpreted by native speakers. Gordon (1987) cites the example of the U.S. student who mistook a prompt referring to the excessive amount of waste generated by Americans to mean bodily waste. Obviously, non-native speakers are at greater risk of misinterpreting the prompt. Furthermore, if the prompt presents a problem for native speakers, they are often able to reject the assumptions of the prompt, in effect rewriting it or writing around it to suit themselves rather than to accommodate the position implicitly taken by the prompt or the writing assignment. Non-native speakers may not be able to write around the prompt in this way and may instead force themselves to write on the prompt as they construe it rather than making it their own. ESL students frequently report writing essays for assignments they did not fully understand (Newstetter et al., 1989).

Finally, although U.S. students have probably become accustomed to the idea of first and subsequent drafts of their writing, many international students arrive in writing classes in the United States quite unaccustomed to the idea of writing several drafts. In their home countries they were expected to learn to produce perfect drafts at one sitting, as might be done during exams. (This idea should not be entirely foreign to us, since an obsession with the neatness of a student's paper figured into evaluations of student essays for some time in this country [Faigley, 1989], and perhaps still does in some instances.) Thus, these students' training makes them extremely reluctant to erase, cross out, or insert into their writing, and unless they use word processors, they may waste hours painstakingly recopying texts neatly before turning them in.

Problems with Plagiarism

Beginning at the latest during high school, native students are taught that they must not present someone else's work as their own.[2] Our conceptions of private property and ownership emerge in our writing conventions. We think of what we write as our personal possession, like a car; no one can use our words without express permission and without following certain conventions giving the author credit. By the same token, we value originality. When someone writes something, we expect that they are writing because they have something new and unique to say or at least a new way of saying it. We encourage students to find their own voice, to write from their own experience. Being creative means being innovative, original.

But these attitudes toward originality and toward writing as property do not prevail worldwide. Views of knowledge or of writing as personal property may exist in cultures close to our own, but attitudes may be quite different in other cultural settings. In some places in the world, students are encouraged to learn/memorize the writings of the learned of antiquity and to use those, not their own thoughts, in their writing. For these students, originality in the sense that we use the term may seem immodest and presumptuous. It is possible that these students copy the words and phrases of other writers because the limitations of their range in English cause them to feel that there is no other way to say the same thing. But it is equally true that sometimes students use other authors' texts because they admire the way they are written and feel that changing them would imply that they are trying to improve upon them.

Our attitudes toward plagiarism may also seem quite alien to ESL students. Although most students who come to the United

States to study have been exposed to the idea that our conventions forbid copying word for word from a printed source, strange situations nevertheless arise. Recently, a group of Malaysian students came to see me, upset about failing an American history exam. The teacher accused them of plagiarizing on the exam and was punishing them by giving them failing grades. They, however, maintained they had not plagiarized. They knew what plagiarism was, they said, and they had not copied word for word. They had memorized the textbook and repeated that back on the exam, convinced that they had not, in fact, violated our rules against plagiarism. Clearly, it is important to explain to these students our alien attitudes toward plagiarism.

Another related area is copying from each other. While there is pressure on students in the United States to allow weaker students to copy the work of stronger students, there is also a lot of energy working against this; whether or not students should do so is a moral question that is discussed in high schools, and students are taught not to let anyone copy from them. The attitude a lot of ESL students come with, though, is that people should help each other, work together in a group. If your cousin asks to copy your work, you may feel under a moral imperative to let that person do it, to help your cousin or the student from your village or your home country.

In this regard, as Cowan (1978) points out, we have in our educational system a fair number of exams and evaluations of students; in other systems, however, students advance to the next level of course work or are admitted to academic rather than vocational high schools, or in some cases even elementary schools that will lead to academic high schools, all on the basis of a single exam. The students taking these exams are under extreme pressure to pass, and getting help from a classmate may make the difference between one type of future existence and another. Thus, it is very difficult to resist asking for and giving that help, particularly if the moral imperative against doing so is not as strong as the imperative to cooperate and care for your own.

Use of the Dictionary

Because they are easy to carry around, ESL students tend to use tiny bilingual dictionaries that often give bizarre translations of words or at best give several different translation options but without any context. So ESL students may have no idea which of the several possible translations might be appropriate for the context they are working on. One student referred to the difference between "the rules of English and the *vivid* language." I finally realized that the word he wanted was *living*, but his dictionary listed *vivid*, *living*, and several others as possible translations of a Chinese word. He probably knew the word *living* and didn't think it fit this context, where it is used somewhat metaphorically, so he chose a word he did not know, hoping that it would correctly express his idea.

Tiny bilingual dictionaries may do students the greatest disservice, but students resort to them because sometimes the meanings given in English-English dictionaries only create more confusion, making use in the definitions of words which students know no better than they do the original word they looked up. Furthermore, since native speakers do not need this information, dictionaries written for native speakers have no reason to indicate how a word is used, for example, if a verb takes a gerund as a verb complement (avoid *doing* something) or an infinitive (expect *to do* something) or an infinitive with a second subject (require *someone to do* something). (See Chapter 9, which discusses the types of errors ESL students make.) Yet this type of information is essential to correct sentence formation. Fortunately, there are two learner dictionaries which do address these questions that teachers can point out to ESL students: *Oxford Student's Dictionary of American English* and *Longman's Dictionary of American English*. Another dictionary, *The BBI Combinatory Dictionary of English*, does not give definitions but does list collocations — for example, which prepositions to use after certain words: *believe in, afraid of, rely on.*

Another, opposite kind of problem with using a dictionary is that many students come from places where dictionaries do not play a big part in education, sometimes simply because looking up a word is so difficult. Arabic vocabulary, for example, is built on tripartite consonant roots, so the words for *book, school, student,* and *teacher* might all be built on the letters *k-t-b* in combination with different vowels. To look up a word in the dictionary, it is necessary to know what that consonant root is. This would be like looking up the word *misconceive* under the Latin root *cept* (Thompson-Panos and Thomas-Ruzic, 1983). Dictionaries are simply too hard to use, their use apparently is not encouraged in some educational systems, and as a result, some students never come to see the advantage of referring to a dictionary in English either.

Use of the Library

Libraries play an important role in education in this country; most high schools have them, most municipalities of any size have them;

libraries often run children's reading programs. So most students who end up in college have a fair degree of familiarity with libraries. This is not necessarily true of ESL students. In some cases, these students may come from countries with few libraries or with libraries reserved for scholars, not students, and certainly not young students. But even when this is not the case, in different parts of the world people rely less on libraries than on book stores for reading and even research material. In teaching English to literature majors in a university in Colombia which had a library on the university campus, I was surprised to learn that none of my students had ever even been there. Many of these highly educated students, who read a great deal in both Spanish and English, had never used a card catalog and did not know how to use one. Thus, teachers of ESL students may need to help orient students like these to the use of libraries.

Conclusion

ESL students are a diverse group, and most of them have spent many years in educational systems different from our own to varying degrees. They come with different assumptions about writing, perhaps about everything. As they become acclimatized to the new educational system in which they find themselves, they will require the patience and help of their teachers. We can help them by anticipating some of their problems and by being willing to accommodate some of their special needs.

In making writing assignments it would seem to make sense to question ESL students about how familiar they are and how comfortable they feel with a topic. It might also help to verify, particularly early in the term, how they are representing a given task to themselves to confirm that their interpretation of the task is accurate.

Keeping an open mind in responding to the content of their writing seems particularly important since their assumptions about the world may be quite alien, even offensive. As in dealings with all students, we walk a narrow line between respecting students' rights to their own views and vigorously challenging their unexamined assumptions. The assumptions of ESL students may be not only different from our own but also built on realities we have no experience with. Assumptions of native students are challenged in college within a context that remains familiar. When those of international students are challenged, they may be absolutely alone in defending their views, as was the case with the Indian student described earlier in the class discussion of the Flannery O'Connor short story. No doubt his countrymen, and probably many of his countrywomen as well, would have supported his views, but he found himself in the painful position of having no one to turn to who might vouch for his version of reality. Life in a new culture assaults these students from many directions. It is important to remain sensitive to their added burdens.

While these added burdens on the students may perforce impose on teachers the need to remain especially alert to signs of strain, there are rewards. ESL students often exhibit an admirable and refreshing commitment to task. Much of their writing is a joy to read, filled with startling uses of English and details, sometimes fascinating, sometimes horrifying, of their lives in other worlds. But most compelling may be the bracing reminder to ourselves and, in mixed native/non-native writing classes, to our native students of the relativity of our own realities.

Chapter Seven

L2 Composing
Strategies and Perceptions

ESL students bring with them to writing classes their diverse personal, cultural, political, and educational histories. The one feature which they share and which sets them apart from average native English-speaking students, however, is that they all have another (maybe more than one other) language besides English in which they are able to function. This bilingualism has implications for the cognitive writing processes ESL students bring to composing in an L2, and these implications need to be taken into account in the writing classroom. But when ESL students first began appearing in numbers in English-medium institutions, their writing needs were considered primarily language learning needs. Thus, researchers and teachers interested in determining appropriate pedagogies for these students focused, not on their writing processes, but on their language learning processes. Since bilingualism — that is, language — distinguished ESL students from native English-speaking students, it seemed obvious that ESL writing classes needed to focus on language.

In the early 1980s, L2 writing classes were still emphasizing linguistic competence as a prerequisite to learning to write. Difficulties with writing were generally addressed through language practice activities, and actual composing (creating through writing) was often postponed until students had more or less mastered English syntax and morphology.

But when research on L2 composing processes finally began in the early 1980s, they revealed basic similarities between L1 and L2 writers, concluding that as far as composing processes were concerned, the distinction to be made was not between L1 and L2 writers but between experienced and inexperienced writers. Inexperienced L2 writers used generally ineffective processes similar to those used by inexperienced L1 writers, and experienced L2 writers, regardless of their linguistic proficiency (at least among those already fairly advanced in English), used processes similar to those of experienced L1 writers (Zamel, 1983). As a result of these kinds of findings, researchers began endorsing imitation of L1 writing classroom practices in ESL writing classrooms. Research findings which emphasized the similarity between L1 and L2 writing supported the idea that L2 writing classes needed to become less focused on language and more focused on composing, just as L1 classes were doing. Since their writing processes were so similar to those of native speakers, it was assumed that ESL students could and should be taught in the same way as L1 writers were being taught.

Similarities

An important finding of L2 composing process research has been that when non-native writers write in English, they are able to rely on strategies that they employ in their L1 writing. ESL students who are expert writers in their L1 are able to plan, to hold in mind concerns about gist while considering organizational possibilities, and to compare text with intentions; they have access to those same skills and strategies when composing in L2 (Cumming, 1989; Zamel, 1983). In both their L1 and in English, experienced ESL writers have in mind some idea of what they hope to achieve in their writing, construct plans to achieve those goals, and seem able to discern when the goals have been met to their own satisfaction. Thus, they seem to function in much the same way as expert writers in English function (Cumming, 1989).

Interestingly, the ability to engage these effective strategies appears to be independent of the writers' L2 language proficiency, at least with intermediate and advanced learners of English (Cumming, 1989). In other words, while language proficiency may have an additive effect on the quality of a text, language proficiency in and of itself appears to be an independent factor in the students' ability to write well in L2. Expert L2 writers with less language proficiency are not impeded in their use of global cognitive strategies in writing by their lesser ability in language; by the same token, inexperienced writers with greater fluency in English are not able to tap into more effective writing processes by virtue of their greater proficiency in English. It is not at all unusual for ESL students, particularly immigrant students, who are quite fluent in spoken English to have trouble writing. After all, being a native English speaker does not guarantee an ability to write. But more importantly, this finding implies that to improve their writing, L2 writers do not need more work with language but rather with writing, since *lack* of fluency in English does not appear to impede employment of effective writing strategies — at least not in any fundamental way.[1] It is possible that more attention to language results in less attention to more global writing functions and therefore restricts the amount, though not the quality, of planning that an L2 writer can do (Jones and Tetroe, 1987).[2]

While it might not be obvious how much of their L1 writing ability is available to L2 writers, it does seem intuitively clear that those who never learned effective writing strategies in L1 cannot employ them in L2 despite a great deal of fluency in L2. Like their native English-speaking counterparts, inexperienced ESL writers have more difficulty knowing where their writing is going and keeping larger chunks of meaning in mind as they write. Like basic writers, they appear to use a "what next?" approach to organizing their material (Cumming, 1989; Bereiter and Scardamalia, 1987), stopping at the end of a thought unit and puzzling over what they might add to it. Whether intermediate or advanced users of English, these inexperienced writers seem to attend to details of language use as they compose and, in experimental writing protocols, may refer to learned rules of English grammar or mechanics, relying on Monitor use (see Chapter 2) to push their writing along (Cumming, 1989; Jones, 1985).

For the writing teacher, then, helping inexperienced ESL writers improve their writing should be quite similar to teaching inexperienced native writers. It may be more difficult to determine immediately which ESL writers are proficient writers in their L1s and which are not, but since their writing processes are similar to those of native English speakers, they can probably benefit from many of the same teaching techniques.

Differences

The idea that L1 and L2 writing processes are basically similar has now won general acceptance; nevertheless, that important differences also exist seems to be a given among ESL teachers and researchers as well. Thus, as research has evolved in the study of L2 composing processes, the focus is shifting from similarities between L1 and L2 writers to differences. Unfortunately, there is still not very much information on the nature of these differences, and a clear picture of these students' writing processes is only just beginning to emerge.

Studies of cognition as information processing suggest that cognitive resources are limited, and if processing capacity is being used for one function, other functions can only make use of whatever capacity is left over (Bereiter and Scardamalia, 1987). It seems obvious, then, that if students must use part of their cognitive capacity to focus on language because they are not familiar with that language, other functions, perhaps higher functions of organization, cannot be engaged at full capacity. For ESL writers, this may explain research that shows that ESL students who can plan in their L1 can also plan in writing in their L2 but not as extensively or elaborately (Jones and Tetroe, 1987). *[handwritten margin note: limited cognitive resources — some devoted to language]*

Other interesting observations of how L2 writers work and how their strategies differ from those of L1 writers have been uncovered. Bereiter and Scardamalia (1987) noticed that inexperienced writers stopped at the end of sentences to reread what they had written and to puzzle over "What next?" but Raimes (1985) observed some of her inexperienced ESL writers doing something different. They did not stop at the end of sentences but often plunged immediately into the beginning of the next sentence and, once there, ground to a halt, unable either to continue with that sentence or to abandon that beginning. The inflexibility of refusing to abandon a fruitless beginning may be characteristic of basic writers, L1 or L2, but what makes these hesitations different, as Raimes points out, is that they occur at this odd point in the sentence. This suggests that the students have, in fact, decided the direction of the next thought but do not have the means for carrying out their plans. They may be better able to plan than basic writers but less able to put their plans into action. *[handwritten margin note: Better able to plan, but less able to put them into action]*

It is also possible that as these L2 students are writing, their short-term memories are taxed in such a way that they can remember only the first words of their plans for the next sentence, with the gist of the idea slipping away. Commenting on broader concerns of text construction, Freedman, Pringle, and Yalden (1983) assert that "constraints of writing, without full proficiency, in a second language may impose psychological limitations on people's abilities to conceptualize their intended meaning and its organization as discourse" (10).

Another difference observed between ESL students and L1 writers (including ESL students writing in their own L1) is related to word choice. While a teacher looking at a student's writing may see errors in word choice, what is not obvious is the tortured

*Word
choice*

indecision some ESL students display as they try to determine the appropriate word to use in a given context. L1 writers appear to rehearse word choices, listening to how chosen words resonate with the writers' intended meanings and perhaps even developing a different perspective on the intended meaning as a result of what a word brings with it. L2 writers rehearse far less in their L2, even though the very same writers do rehearse in their L1 (Arndt, 1987). Thus, L2 writers are perhaps prevented from using a strategy in L2 which they do use well in L1. No doubt it is the lack of resonance that L2 words have for these writers that precludes rehearsing. Instead, dissatisfied with word choices they have made, yet limited in the alternatives available to them, these students revise their word choices over and over, spending a great deal of time on single words, unable to decide which one of the scant number of choices available to them is the correct or most appropriate one. Clearly, there is no question here of words bringing further, richer possible interpretations of the writers' intentions. Rather, these words stubbornly expose only a fraction of their meanings to L2 writers and force them to struggle in the dark, a struggle that remains hidden from the teacher.

L2 Advantages

Despite all these added difficulties caused by lack of proficiency in L2, ESL students' proficiency in L1 can also be a resource not available to monolinguals. Many writing protocols have shown ESL students switching to their L1s as they plan and write in English. They may be missing the resonance of words in English, but they can apparently use the resonances which words in their native languages have for them as touchstones to spur their thinking along and to verify the exact meanings they intend. Thus, contrary to popular belief, thinking in the L1 should not necessarily be avoided while composing in L2. Both skilled and unskilled L2 writers have been shown to use this technique to their advantage, even going so far as to write sections of their texts in their L1 and later translate them into English with positive results (Friedlander, 1990; Cumming, 1989; Zamel, 1982).

*Why would
you do
This?*

Yet, regardless of what they may do in practice, some L2 writers, like many language teachers, recommend thinking entirely in English (Zamel, 1982). In fact, the picture appears to be more complicated than simply encouraging or discouraging L1 use in L2 writing. While the use of L1 seems to benefit some writers, the use of L1 by writers more proficient in English may give their writing a foreign sound that they avoid when using only L2 to plan and generate their texts (Lay, 1982). Thus, it simply is not yet clear whether or not writing teachers should recommend a strategy of recourse to L1 for ESL students who are having trouble.

To further complicate the issue of L1 use in L2 writing, research shows that the amount of L1 that ESL students use depends in part on the topic that they are addressing (Burtoff, 1983; Johnson, 1985; Lay, 1982). In these studies, students tended to use L1 more frequently when writing about events that took place during a period when these students were functioning in L1 or when they had originally learned about their topics in L1. Thus, topics which presumably are stored in the students' L1 may be particularly beneficial ones to write on for some students (up to a certain level of English proficiency) and particularly detrimental to write on for other students (more proficient in English).

Inexperienced ESL writers may have other advantages over their native English-speaking counterparts. Early in the study of ESL student composing processes, during the time when researchers were looking for similarities, they expected that one of the great impediments to fluent writing would be, as it is for native writers, a focus primarily on form rather than on meaning. Later studies did reveal that when L2 writers focus on form, they do so at the expense of meaning. However, surprisingly, it soon became clear that many ESL writers did not, in fact, focus on form nearly as much as it had been assumed. The long pauses between stretches of writing typical of ESL writers turned out to reflect, more often than not, a search for meaning rather than for errors in grammar or mechanics. While ESL students often express a desire to write error-free English (Leki, 1991b), they apparently do not allow a concern with error to prevent their plugging away at meaning. Clearly, error is simply not as stigmatizing for ESL students writing in an L2 as it is for native English-speaking basic writers writing in L1; even inexperienced ESL writers are able to focus on meaning. (See Chapter 3 for a further discussion of attitudinal differences between ESL and basic writers.) In fact, errors may be so much less stigmatizing for ESL students that they may not bother to edit carefully, simply expecting their teachers to correct their errors (Raimes, 1985; Radecki and Swales, 1988).

Perhaps for this reason, ESL writers feel freer to write, and, as a result, in research situations, have produced more text than might have been expected given what basic writers produce under similar conditions. In one study, although ESL writers typically produced only one draft of a piece of writing under experimental conditions whereas native basic writers produced several, the ESL writers produced more words and spent more time working than their native speaker colleagues (Raimes, 1985). Raimes concludes that ESL students generally exhibit a great deal of commitment to the task of learning to write, and learning English, a conclusion many classroom teachers would attest to as well.

But to produce the numbers of words that they manage, L2 writers need considerably more time than native speakers need. The students in Raimes's study (1985) did not use this time to edit at the micro-text level or to revise at the macro-text level by producing multiple drafts. ESL students seem to be using their time to formulate ideas in their L2, "to marshal the vocabulary they need to make their own background knowledge accessible to them in their L2" (Raimes, 1985, 250), and to allow meanings of words to resonate with meanings they intend. If this is the case, single drafts and long pauses while writing perhaps do not need to be remedied through the fluency exercises used to encourage native English-speakers to write rapidly and continuously, forgetting concerns about textual details for the sake of meaning. ESL students are already attending to meaning. But their single drafts may suggest that their language limitations make it "more problematic to write a lot, to sustain the effort of writing, and to analyze the product in order to make changes" (250). Thus, they need more time; in fact, Raimes (1985) concludes that ESL students need more of everything: more time, more contact with English, more opportunity to read and write (248).

L2 Diversity

Research into the composing processes of ESL students provides one more particularly interesting, and perhaps curious, finding that seems to distinguish these writers from native English-speaking writers whose composing processes have been observed. While researchers into the composing processes of native English writers have been able to differentiate between experienced and inexperienced L1 writers based on patterns of strategies they use to produce text, with L2 writers the picture appears more complex and varied. Unlike Perl's (1979) inexperienced L1 writers, who showed a great deal of similarity in the writing strategies they exhibited, the composing behaviors of Raimes's (1985) inexperienced L2 writers were not consistent. Some wrote recursively, some did not; some reread their texts many times, others did not (one reread her text three times, for example, another fifty-one times) (249). Furthermore, a study of post-graduate Chinese students revealed that while they were all able to use L1 writing strategies in English writing, they employed very different strategies (Arndt, 1987). One created an elaborate plan before beginning to write; another was an emergent planner (Cumming, 1989), thinking through his ideas as they appeared before him on the page; another continuously tested and altered what was appearing on the page to make it conform to intentions which she apparently kept in her head; still another wrote fluently and easily, changing her text while rereading what she had written rather than while writing (Arndt, 1987, 261). In other words, while it may be possible to make some generalizations about composing patterns of L2 writers, as yet it seems that we do not know enough about them to be able to characterize them with much confidence, exactitude, or completeness.

This inability to characterize L2 writers may well be less a reflection of actual diversity (although they are surely diverse) than a quirk of the research conducted to date on L2 composing processes. Findings are inconclusive and sometimes contradictory because most composing process research has been based on case studies focusing on very few students, probably only a total number of between 100 and 150 (Krapels, 1990, 50). If fairly wide variations are seen in small groups of six to eight students, 100 or 150 subjects are probably not enough to show dominant patterns rather than individual variations. (For a review of composing process studies, see Krapels, 1990; for a critique of L2 composing process studies, see Silva, 1989). In any case, one pattern does emerge fairly clearly from this research: L2 writers are not entirely different from L1 writers at the same level of competence in writing, nor are they exactly the same. In terms of pedagogy, then, it appears that we can and should use successful techniques from L1 writing classes to teach writing to L2 students, *but* we also need to keep in mind that these techniques may need to be adjusted for ESL students. And certainly, notions about how much ESL students can accomplish in a given period of time must remain flexible — how much an L2 writer can produce, how long it will take to produce that amount, and, most importantly, how long it will take L2 writers to show improvement both in language and in writing.

ESL Students' Perceptions of Writing in English

Another relatively untouched area of L2 writing research is the differences ESL students themselves perceive between writing in their first and second languages, yet this information can potentially help writing teachers make the task of writing in L2 easier. In discussing writing in English, Silva's (forthcoming[3]) ESL students, sophisticated and articulate in their L1s, poignantly voice their frustration at the mismatch between their sense of their writing prowess in their L1s and the inadequacy and inferiority of what they can accomplish in English. Commenting on writing in their L1s, these students say:

> Writing in Chinese is just as easy as talking. (1)
>
> My sentences, just like the ink in my pen, come out naturally. (6)
>
> When I write texts in Chinese, I can chose different words to express [the] same meaning, depending on my feeling and mood. (12)

Students say that they can concentrate on the topic, style, and text structure in L1, that they write long, complex sentences. None of this is true for these students writing in English.

Instead, they express disappointment that they must focus on finding the right words, forms, and word orders in English and that they must sometimes resort to writing out complex ideas in their L1 and then translating this text into English. In English, writing is more "time consuming ... less fluent ... less sophisticated (with simpler words [and] shorter [, simpler] sentences) and less expressive of the writers' thoughts and intentions" (5).

Lack of vocabulary plagues these students. One avoids unfamiliar words for fear of choosing incorrectly, fully aware that, as a result, "the article becomes wordy and powerless" (5). Others lament that they do not know the connotations of words, their nuances in English, and that their "deeper meanings" are then neglected. They have problems with idioms and exceptions. One student sadly admits: "I have to give up some good ideas for I can not find the available words" (12). This problem of limited vocabularies comes into perspective better when we consider that "the average English—native speaker college student has a passive reading and listening vocabulary of around 150,000 words. It would take bilingual learners [i.e., ESL students] four years to acquire such a passive vocabulary *if* they could learn forty words a day 365 days a year! Most researchers claim students can learn around seven new words per day" (Murray, 1989, 77).

Beyond the problem of a generally small vocabulary, these students also face the problem of a limited range of vocabulary. Arndt's students (1987) complained that the only English they had been exposed to was technical textbook English; although they were fairly proficient users of this English, their exposure to English was narrow, resulting in inability to discriminate between and exploit varying registers of language. Murray's bilingual immigrant students (1989) experienced the same problem in the opposite direction. They were quite fluent in the everyday English language use of the street but had had little exposure to academic or technical uses of English. (This fact is yet another reason not to assume that the length of time spent in an English-speaking country correlates well with a student's writing, or even language, abilities.)

Sometimes rather than simply expanding on what they already know about writing by learning more, these ESL students face the chore of unlearning previously successful strategies. For one student (Silva, forthcoming), the first thing that comes to mind when beginning an assignment is an appropriate proverb, yet he knows that proverbs are not typically found in academic English writing; another naturally gravitates towards parables but realizes that these are difficult to translate into English and that even if translation were possible, the parables would not have the same effect.

These students see clearly that their relationship with their audience is transformed by writing in English. One student says she cannot write well for her English readers because she does not know much about them (5); another says she does not feel she shares a common understanding with them (7); still another consistently feels unsure about the level of formality to adopt with her L2 audience (9). Again, often their culturally induced inclinations about how to communicate appropriately with their audience must be resisted. A Chinese audience would expect "citations of historical events" rather than data and rational arguments to support a point (7). A Japanese audience expects diffidence, indirectness:

> For example, when I write an application letter to the scholarship committee as an English assignment, I wrote "I would be a successful student." In Japan I could never say such a thing. To appeal directly has almost an opposite effect. (7)

> [In business letters, Japanese writers] have a tendency to write unnecessarily long and formalized introductory remarks, in which they humble themselves and state as often as they can that they are not able to write their essay and thank as many people as they can. Japanese simply go through the introductory remarks, but this confuses American people because they question why this author is writing this essay if he thinks he is not able to write the essay. (10)

Another student finds English writing crude and complains in frustration:

> The kind of writing the teacher wants . . . is stupid. It is so childish. All he wanted was example example example, concrete, concrete concrete. . . . I can't understand why the reader cannot infer? Why do we have to be so obvious? (Newstetter et al., 1989)

Silva finds that, in general, these students have fewer options, sometimes feeling that their only sense of security comes from what they have learned about grammar.[4] One student remarks: "Grammar is the only tool that I can use in writing English essays" (6). Even understanding an assignment takes more time than it would in L1 (4). These students know that writing in an L2 imposes additional burdens. What they can handle with ease in L1, like ink coming out of a pen, becomes an irritating obstacle in L2, perhaps something like a right-handed person suddenly having to eat, write, and manipulate objects of all kinds with only the left hand.

As a result of this added burden, students often express their frustration at the relationship between the amount of time they require to complete academic tasks and the quality of their final products. They complain that even though they begin academic assignments in plenty of time, they often feel pressed to finish the work by the deadline and may not have time to review it (Jones, 1985). While the students themselves may recognize that the quality of some piece of work is not up to their own normal standards of excellence, they nevertheless experience keen disappointment when their work, which has required so much time and effort, is evaluated by a teacher as weak or inadequate.

Conclusion

Hidden behind the texts that ESL students produce is once again the great diversity of the ESL student population. Krapels (1990) points out: "The L2 composition class may represent at least half a dozen strikingly different cultures, very different educational back-grounds, ages ranging from sixteen to sixty, and very different needs for being able to write in a foreign language" (45). Their composing processes differ to some degree from those of L1 writers and apparently from those of other L2 writers as well. We know little about the composing processes of students for whom English may be a third or fourth language and what further complications, benefits, or strategies these additional languages account for.

When ESL students appear in writing classes, it is difficult to know exactly how much training in writing they have received in their L1 or how expert they may be at writing in their L1. Little research has been reported on writing strategies in other languages, and to some degree, composing process researchers have assumed a universal of good writing strategies. Can we count on that universality as we teach our students to write? That is, if students are experienced in writing in their L1s, could this experience itself prove to be a complicating element in their writing in L2? (See Chapter 8, "Contrastive Rhetoric.")

If ESL students are placed into writing classes based on language proficiency, we may have some picture of their language abilities, but these abilities are not unambiguously correlated to writing abilities. Fluency in language may be obscuring lack of experience with writing and even lack of cognitive academic development, a particular problem for some immigrant students; or, on the other hand, lack of fluency in English may mislead us into underestimating a student's writing abilities and experience.

However diverse these students may be, L2 writing research shows that L2 students share a need for more time to accomplish their writing tasks. If ESL students need more time than native students to accomplish the same task, they are obviously expending more energy than their native English-speaking classmates are. It is probably the need to expend more time and energy on both reading and writing, and probably on listening and speaking as well, which puts ESL students at the greatest disadvantage in English-medium classes with native speakers. If ESL students are going to have any chance at all of surviving in writing classes, writing teachers need to remain sensitive to the excess burden placed on ESL students working in English. What might be a reasonable time limit within which native students can be expected to complete a reading or writing assignment is most likely *un*reasonable for ESL students, whether in or out of class. If it seems reasonable for native speakers to be able to produce five essays or 3,000 words in a semester, the same requirement for ESL students is clearly unfair since the ESL students must expend more time, effort, and energy to accomplish the same tasks. Extending time limits or reducing work loads, far from lowering standards, as some fret, merely creates more equalized working conditions. If no other accommodation to the special needs of L2 writers can be made, at the very least, extension of time limits and reduction of work loads for ESL writers, experienced or inexperienced, are absolutely essential adjustments.

Chapter Eight

Contrastive Rhetoric

ESL teachers are sometimes able to identify the nationality of a student writer just by looking at that student's writing. Certain handwriting styles, grammatical errors, or recurring themes are typical of students from particular cultural and linguistic backgrounds. A more subtle identifier is the way the ideas in a piece of writing are developed. Sometimes ESL writing seems odd not because of errors, but because it gives the native reader an ineffable sense that the writing misses the point. But the way a point is appropriately made in writing in one language differs from the way it is done in another; the rules for presenting ideas and strategies for explaining or defending them that may seem self-evident are not completely interchangeable across cultures.

What is relevant/irrelevant, and to some extent, what is logical/illogical, what constitutes proof of an argument, what an argument is, who may construct an argument, and even who may write are culturally determined. Consider, for example, the fact that distinctions like relevant/irrelevant are so much a part of a distinctly *academic* American discourse community that those distinctions are not obvious even for American college freshmen, let alone nonnatives of the language and culture.

The study of contrastive rhetorics is as old as written translation, but contrastive rhetoric studies of interest to writing teachers began with Robert Kaplan's study (1966) of some six hundred L2 student essays in the 1960s. From examining texts ESL students had written in English, Kaplan concluded that students from different language backgrounds systematically developed their ideas in writing in patterns different from those that would appear natural in English. His little diagrams of how different cultural groups supposedly organize ideas in writing are well known in ESL circles and represent Kaplan's initial intuitions about cross-cultural textual development.

Kaplan's diagrammatic depiction of what he took to be typical Romance and Slavic language paragraphs begins as an arrow headed straight down but soon deviates into zigzags down the page, representing digressions. Arabic is represented by a series of parallel lines linked with dotted diagonal lines. The "Oriental" pattern Kaplan draws is a spiral gradually closing in on the middle of the page. None of these looked like English patterns.

Kaplan's description of the typical English pattern of development comes from rhetoric handbooks of the 1960s. His drawing representing the English paragraph is an arrow going straight from the top of the paragraph to the bottom. English rhetoric, in this account, is direct and straightforward.

But beginning at least in the 1970s, researchers studying English rhetoric showed how little the texts of professional writers conformed to the school book versions of good English writing (Braddock, 1974). That message did not get through to ESL teachers for some time, however. Instead, Kaplan's diagrammatic depictions of the rhetoric of English and other languages became quite popular, informing the teaching of ESL/EFL writing for years. They have been widely reprinted, including in ESL composition textbooks, and taken by many as accurate depictions of how different cultures write.

Kaplan meant his work to be exploratory, but perhaps because these little diagrams are so clear and simple, they have led some teachers and students directly to the wrong-headed notion that rhetorical patterns reveal innate *thought* processes of other cultures. Furthermore, the depiction of the English paragraph as a straight line has been equated with English as logical, and, by inescapable implication (at least to those who value this version of logic), superior, while the written expressions of other cultures seem somehow twisted or scattered.

But, of course, rules and strategies for presenting ideas are not innate, universal, or strictly logical. They are rhetorical, and rhetorical preferences and conventions are taught in schools. Writing is not natural but rather "provoked activity" (Widdowson, 1983, 44). After all, while many children can already read when they start school and many read outside school for entertainment, few can write when they enter school and except for letters and lists, few write outside school. In other words, writing for most school age people is nearly always school sponsored, and like everything taught in schools, the teaching of writing and rhetorical patterns reflects

social, economic, and political realities, not natural mental processes
or psychological capacities.

Interestingly, not many cultures appear to teach rhetorical patterns directly, as we do in our schools. In fact, while English bulges
with rhetoric handbooks, few other languages have handbooks or
courses specifically devoted to teaching writing. (See Kachru, 1984;
Eggington, 1987; and Hinds, 1987, for discussions of India, Korea,
and Japan, respectively.) France seems to be one exception. Secondary school students are directly trained to construct arguments
following a clear pattern — thesis, antithesis, synthesis — and in
baccalaureate exams are apparently expected to reproduce this
pattern quite rigidly (Bassetti, 1990).[1]

Nevertheless, even if rhetorical patterns are not directly taught,
it is clear that young school children's writing style is formed by
reactions to the writing they produce in school and reflects the
currently prevailing preferences. And these preferences shift. A
great deal of evidence shows those shifts in English (Faigley, 1989)
and in other languages from one time period to the next. Chinese,
for example, is said to be currently undergoing such a shift from a
reader-responsible to writer-responsible rhetoric (Hinds, 1987). (See
below for a discussion of these terms.) Cultures evolve writing
styles appropriate to their own histories and the needs of their
societies.

It is important to stress the relatively arbitrary nature of rhetoric
because all rhetorics seem to want to claim for themselves that they
are self-evidently logical. Thus, texts that do not follow the rules of
that rhetoric, and the students who write these texts, are judged
illogical when, in fact, logic is not really the issue, but rather
rhetorical strategies. Furthermore, the problems created by the variety
of rhetorics are particularly insidious because differences in rhetorical styles are not as readily visible as errors in vocabulary,
grammar, or punctuation. Thus, no one really speaks of errors in
English rhetoric but instead about the writer's lack of logic or of
ability to think.[2] To compound the problem for ESL students, most
non-native speakers of English stop formal study of English abroad
well before the issue of contrastive rhetoric is addressed in a language
class. So, they may remain completely unaware, as of course most
English speakers are, that there are differences in rhetorical styles.
As a result, the causes of breakdowns in communication cannot
be easily pinpointed, and both the writer and the reader become
frustrated.

But the greatest danger of failing to regard rhetorical logic as
socially *constructed* rather than as a reflection of innate thought
processes probably comes from those who are familiar enough with
another culture (ironically, often natives of that culture) to feel

justified in interpreting that culture to others, sometimes falling
into a smugness bordering on racism as they describe the "national
character" that supposedly naturally gives rise to a particular
rhetoric. One writer, for example, claims: "English is tailored for
egalitarianism. When speaking English, the Japanese must think
democratically. This is not easy. . . . The Japanese do not think in
terms of systematic thought; this requires logic. They prefer emotion
and intuition, the experience of the moment. And their language
was shaped to serve this predilection" (Edamatsu, 1978, 18). The
same kinds of borderline racist remarks have described the language
of Chinese, Latins, Poles, and, needless to say, women and African-
Americans.

A simplistic application of the findings of contrastive rhetoric
has created other problems. Before a process orientation to writing
pedagogy developed in ESL, and, with it, greater sensitivity to the
complexity of writing tasks, it was perhaps enthusiasm for simple
answers that resulted in prescriptions for writing in English. If
preferred rhetorical patterns can be identified, then all that is necessary is the imitation of those patterns. This kind of thinking has
sometimes led process-oriented ESL writing teachers and researchers
to disdain the findings of contrastive rhetoric studies as inevitably
leading to prescriptive teaching. While the findings of contrastive
rhetoric do not necessarily lead to formulas for writing, some ESL
writing students may expect writing teachers to provide simple
answers to the problems of appropriate organization and development of ideas in English writing and, like anyone inexperienced in
a particular skill, will cling to whatever insights they may be given
along these lines.

Some ESL researchers (Mohan and Lo, 1985) dispute the notion
that contrastive rhetoric findings have any application in writing
classrooms on other grounds. They argue that the "deviant" patterns
which appeared in the writing of Chinese students in the analyses
of Kaplan and of others after him may have been examples of the
writing of the inexperienced and did not reproduce rhetorical
patterns of their native cultures. In other words, they suggest that
ESL writers need the same kind of writing instruction as any other
inexperienced writer. They are not transferring alien writing patterns
to English; they have no developed writing patterns, alien or otherwise; and, therefore, contrastive analyses of rhetorical patterns are
irrelevant to writing classrooms.

But there are several reasons to believe that contrastive rhetoric
is not completely irrelevant. Since even different discourse communities within a single culture have different expectations of
writing (for example, preferred length of sentences, choice of vocabulary, acceptability of using first person, extent of using passive

voice, degree to which writers are permitted to interpret, amount of metaphorical language accepted), it makes some sense that different cultures would have different expectations of writing, and that students, who have lived in their own cultures, gone to school, and read books, would have built up structural schemata reflecting those expectations, that is, would have internalized patterns of discourse prevalent in their cultures (Carrell and Eisterhold, 1983; Connor, 1984). This would seem to be the case particularly for graduate students, who must certainly have well-developed discourse schemata in their own languages and more than likely in their academic disciplines. Finally, evidence exists that writing skills do transfer across languages (Hall, 1990; Cumming, 1989; Jones and Tetroe, 1987).

If we can assume that different cultures do present written ideas in different ways, that members of a culture internalize those patterns of development, and that students transfer what they know about one writing situation to another, then a familiarity with contrastive rhetoric studies will help writing teachers understand the difficulties ESL students may have with writing and perhaps the origin of those difficulties. It will also help teachers recognize when students' problems arise from an attempt to apply previously learned writing strategies to new writing contexts.

The writing strategies ESL students use in response to culturally patterned rhetorical constraints may seem illogical, digressive, or circuitous to an English-speaking reader. ESL students may use rhetorical strategies that strike academic readers as odd: "the freshman composition essay that is highly philosophical and generalized instead of being highly specific and personalized as the professor expected; the political science paper that has elaborate language and irrelevant materials that do not address 'the point'; the research paper that has been copied from one or two sources" (Reid, 1989, 221).

The problem lies in the disjuncture of the writer's and the reader's view of what is needed in a text. Part of what it means to share a culture is to share assumptions about reality and knowledge. One of these shared assumptions is an agreement on what constitutes proof of an assertion. English readers learn to be convinced by such evidence as facts, statistics, and illustrations despite our awareness that these proofs cannot, in fact, guarantee truth. English readers do not rely heavily on analogy, an appeal to intuition, the beauty of language, or a reference to opinions of the learned of antiquity. Yet conventions of argumentation in other cultures may require precisely that recourse to analogy, intuition, beauty, or shared communal wisdom. Thus, a misfit may occur between the writer's and the reader's sense of how to argue a point.

Another culturally determined calculation involved in constructing a text centers on textual coherence. Coherence in a text is less a quality of the text itself than an accurate assessment by the writer of what the reader can infer from the text. In reading any text, the reader is to some extent called upon to make inferential bridges among the propositions of the text based on the reader's own knowledge of the world. But as Weissberg (1984) points out "what may be an easily identifiable reference for one reader, requiring minimal bridging, may be more obscure for another" (491). In some cases, "the bridging required may be so extensive as to render the [text] incomprehensible" (491). To the extent that members of different cultures do not share the same collective knowledge and experience, the non-native writer may miscalculate the ability of the native reader to construct these inferential bridges.

Not only coherence but actual meaning is at issue. Recent reading theory no longer regards meaning as residing in a text. Instead, schema theory (Carrell, 1983) assumes that the reader actively *constructs* meaning, based on the interaction between the text and the reader's schemata, or patterns of stored knowledge, and proposes that comprehension of a text is a function of the text's ability to activate a reader's schemata. If a text can draw upon a reader's knowledge and experience, it is much more likely to be understood regardless of the linguistic difficulty of the text (including surface level error).

Non-native speakers of English are at a disadvantage when attempting to activate the schemata appropriate for native-speaking readers because they are less likely to be aware of what the native-speaker audience's needs are. Scarcella (1984), for example, found that non-native speakers overspecify in introductions they write, underestimating their reader's knowledge and, as a result, produce information which appears irrelevant or obvious to native speakers. Here is how a fairly proficient non-native user of English began a paper on the economic conditions in her country.

> My name is ———. I come from Taiwan, Republic of China. Taiwan in one part of China, but she split away from mainland China after a civil war in 1950.
>
> The area of Taiwan is about 36,000 square-kilometers, that is pretty small, but our people is diligent and intelligent. We make miracles in both the education and economics during the past years. (683)

This writer did not know what to assume about how much orientation her reader would need. She would almost certainly *not* have thought to orient her reader in the same way if she had been preparing this text for her compatriots. While the issue of assessing and addressing audience needs and of anticipating the amount of inferential bridging a reader can make exists to some extent for all writers, this problem is dramatically exacerbated if reader and writer do not share cultures.

Thus, L2 writing students must make complex evaluations of their new writing contexts and can be expected to use L1 strategies while new discourse patterns are being formed through contact with the target discourse. Modern contrastive rhetoric studies no longer center so much on L2 student writing, having moved to cross-cultural and cross-linguistic analyses of a variety of texts written in L1 often by professional writers (Leki, 1991a). The question for writing teachers, however, remains: What kinds of clues can systematic analyses of the writing in English of ESL students provide writing teachers about these students' native writing strategies? The answer is problematic. Some contrastive rhetoric studies lead to excessively atomized findings. Others lead to excessive generalizations. With these dangers in mind, I have gathered some of the more interesting points contrastive rhetoric researchers have made about the English writing of several general categories of ESL students most frequently represented in U.S. colleges and universities. These summaries are intended only to give teachers a sense of some of the possible differences between the rhetoric we employ and that of a few other cultures.

It may help to start with some generalizations about what native English speakers appear to expect and admire in writing. English expository writing is said to be highly hierarchical. Typically, generalizations are supported by subtopics and specific explanations are directly related to the main point under discussion. English requires fairly explicit indications of the logical links between main topics, subtopics, and subordinated ideas. Directness is usual; digression is not usual. Originality is highly valued. That a writer has something new to say or has a particular case to make is taken for granted. It is also, of course, taken for granted that a person's ideas and language are, in effect, that writer's private property. Hence, our violent reaction to plagiarism.

East Asian

Speakers of other languages, particularly Asian and Middle Eastern languages, do not necessarily share our admiration of directness and explicitness or our aim of providing the reader with the exact implications of what has been stated and with an explanation of exactly how the meaning of statements made in writing relate to each other. In East Asian languages relationships among ideas in a text may remain unspecified. Rather than aiming for directness and explicitness, East Asian writers may work at suggesting. They may prefer to hint at explanations, to grant readers the intelligence to figure out the implications of what has been written and to link the ideas in a text. This style may strike English-speaking readers as circuitous and cause them to feel frustrated at being unable to quickly detect the main point or the development of that point.

A fair amount of work has been done comparing Chinese with English rhetoric and interpreting Chinese economic, social, political, and cultural history for clues about the roots of Chinese style. Studies of ancient Chinese rhetoric have emphasized the value placed on tradition, authority, and harmony (Oliver, 1971). Those who wrote were assumed to know the truth by virtue of the fact that they wrote. The goal of rhetoric was not, as in Western rhetorical tradition, to convince political equals in a public forum of some political position, placing a great deal of emphasis on an individual speaker's ability to reason and to marshal proofs. The Asian tradition that Oliver cites grew out of entirely different political relationships, in which the duty of the rhetor was less to convince than to announce truth and to arrange the propositions of the announcement such that it might be easily and harmoniously agreed upon by referring to communal, traditional wisdom. Language was used not to discover but to uncover truth based on accepted traditional wisdom. Justification for present statements was found not in individual insight but in communal wisdom and past authority. Group unity, consensus, and harmony were emphasized over originality, individuality, analysis, and proof.

(The difference between Western rhetoric's emphasis on individuality and originality and an emphasis on the communality of wisdom and knowledge may account for the great concern in the English tradition about plagiarism, a concern not at all shared in cultures whose rhetorical tradition specifically de-emphasizes individuality.)

A more sinister interpretation of the taste for suggesting rather than directly stating has political roots. The lack of clarity served to protect a writer if then-current rulers were unlikely to appreciate what the writer said. Lack of clarity also helped the ruling elite retain power. They used obfuscation to confuse their audience and remind them that scholars like themselves were superior to the rest of the population (Hu Mi, 1989, personal communication).

However that may be, as a result of the emphasis on tradition and traditional authority, Chinese scholars were recognized as scholars by their ability to learn past teachings. Memorization continues to be highly valued and necessary in order to draw upon the wisdom of the past. Even simply being literate in Chinese requires the memorization of thousands of individual Chinese characters. According to this analysis of Chinese culture, educated Chinese expect to share the same millions of memorized bits of culture. For this reason, cases do not need to be argued the same way as they do in English. Analyses of the English writing of highly educated Chinese fairly proficient in English reveal that typically the Chinese writer provides a series of concrete examples to make a point but may neither state the point nor relate the examples to each other (Matalene, 1985). The writer leaves it to the reader to make inferential bridges among the statements, confident that the reader, also educated, knows exactly what links those examples. For the Chinese writer, this style of writing shows respect for the knowledge, scholarship, and intelligence of the reader. For the English reader accustomed to being shown how an example is linked to a generalization, this approach is perceived as failing to make an argument.

[handwritten margin note: Frank's essay lacks the clear connection in reflection]

In discussing rhetorical elaboration of ideas, Shen (1989) describes Chinese writing as moving from the surface to the core. Good writing in Chinese does not blurt out the main idea but rather builds up to it by "clearing the terrain" first, by discussing ideas which are related to the main idea but which will not be pursued. It may well be that English readers of written thought developed in this style would become confused about exactly what the main idea is.

Graduate students from the People's Republic of China have said this about composing in English and in Chinese:

> It seems that we need a conclusion in English, but we often leave it [off] to let people think when we write in Chinese. We must explain things more clearly and exactly for Americans.

> American audience has to have conclusion; we usually leave it to the reader to sense the conclusion.

> To write for Americans we have to tell everything exactly.

> (Matalene, 1985, 802)

Interestingly, modern Chinese style manuals, just like those in English, encourage Chinese students to write directly and concisely: "'Sometimes when people write compositions, they like to wander about the topic for a long time without talking directly about it.... Essays written in this way have serious problems in organization as well as style' (Hu-bei-sheng Research Team 1973:206).... 'To be concise in writing means that we should not waste our energy in writing anything that is superfluous.... There should be no verbosity and no repetitions. We should write just what we want to say in a concise manner' (*Beijing University* 1973:104–105)" (cited in Mohan and Lo, 1985, 520). In this instance, the Chinese writer is exhorted, just as our students are, to write directly and concisely, but perhaps what constitutes concision and directness varies from one culture to another. It is not unreasonable to speculate that the concrete detail Matalene describes as characteristic of her students' essays might well be what is referred to by the writers of the Chinese style manual as direct and clear. Perhaps writing directly for the Chinese means being specific and concrete. The manual's injunction to avoid repetition might be displayed in a text which draws no conclusion at the end if the conclusion is taken to be obvious from the exposition. Yet the possible repetition implied by an explicit conclusion is expected in English.

Another explanation for the discrepancy between style manuals and apparently preferred writing styles may be that Chinese rhetoric is in transition from a reader-responsible style, in which it is incumbent upon the reader to work to glean meaning from a text, to a writer-responsible style, in which the writer is enjoined to make meaning as explicit as possible (Hinds, 1987). Thus, while style manuals urge young writers to aim for conciseness and directness, the essays rated most highly on entrance exams in Chinese universities remain those with more traditional features like elaborate metaphors and literary references (Jie and Lederman, 1988).

[margin note: shifting from reader responsible to writer responsible]

While both Chinese and Japanese are characterized by English-speaking analysts as indirect in their rhetoric, the Japanese seem to be even more eager than the Chinese to embrace that characterization. Here are some Japanese students' comments on their own prose style:

> [The Japanese] prefer to be modest and polite, what we call an old-fashioned way.

> Our generation has been trained to be able to appreciate our own feelings and an author's intention of writing indirectly. . . . We try to achieve what we call "guessing skill," writing as indirectly as we can and we read a great amount of indirect writing.

> (Liebman-Kleine, 1988)

Hinds (1987) characterizes Japanese writing style as reader-responsible. For successful communication, the reader is required to make many inferential bridges between propositions and to deduce meaning from a text. In Japanese the lack of clear explicit meaning may be a style associated with intelligence and sensitivity.

[margin note: Japanese lack of explicit meaning assoc. w/ intelligence]

Japanese rhetoric has probably undergone more systematic study in this country than has any other. As a result relatively more research data exists supporting anecdotal and intuitive descriptions of modern Japanese prose style. One pattern of Japanese style, which some researchers have claimed to be a basic pattern (Hinds, 1980), consciously repeats the four-part organization of classical Chinese poetry: "First, begin one's argument. Next, develop that. At the point where this development is finished, turn the idea to a subtheme where there is a connection, but not a directly connected association (to the major theme). Last, bring all of this together and reach a conclusion," a summary, or both (Hinds, 1980, 132). A common pattern of organization derived from this basic pattern "is characterized by a decision on the part of the author to select a baseline theme [but one which need not be explicitly expressed] and then to return overtly to this theme before progressing to a different perspective" (133). The repeated return to the baseline theme is intended to reinforce the theme for the reader but is likely to be taken by the English reader as odd repetition, particularly when the theme is never explicitly stated. It is not surprising that the English-speaking reader, accustomed to hierarchically arranged information, might read this approach as vague, as circling around an idea rather than developing it.

Findings of another study (Kobayashi, 1984) of the writing of Japanese and American college students show that Americans systematically choose to present their ideas by beginning with a general statement and moving to specifics; they also used summary statements to reestablish the topic and extend it. The Japanese students showed a marked preference for a specific to general pattern and for relating the text information to the writer's own experience.

In another study (Dennett, 1990), Japanese graduate students who voluntarily enrolled in a technical writing course were asked to describe what they felt characterized good technical writing. Such writing, they said, would engage the emotions through beauty, surprise, and flow. This description is unlikely to correspond to notions about technical writing by native English speakers, who view writing more as a tool than as an object with any aesthetic value of its own. Another series of differences relates to audience awareness. The main concerns of Dennett's U.S. subjects centered on their audience. They worked on their writing to ensure that their argument would be adequately hedged, that their position would remain fairly unassailable, and that the user/reader of the technical text would understand it. The concerns of the Japanese, on the other hand, did not center on audience much. They worked to make the text aesthetically acceptable. Furthermore, they felt that writing was not a discovery process at all but rather that writing should come only *after* thinking (that is, writing itself is not used in order to think more clearly). If a new idea occurred to these writers during the writing, they ignored it and did not try to find a way to incorporate it. (See also Jenkins and Hinds, 1987 for a comparison of business letter writing by English, French, and Japanese speakers.)

Middle Eastern

Way on the other side of spectrum from the diffidence and indirectness of Chinese and Japanese is the prose style of Semitic languages, such as Arabic. Speakers of Arabic are extremely proud of their language. Classical Arabic has served over the centuries as a unifying force among speakers of colloquial Arabics all over the Arabic-speaking world, colloquials which are sometimes mutually unintelligible. But more importantly, Classical Arabic is held in awe as a sacred language and the ideal model because it is the language of the Qur'an.

Researchers (Ostler, 1987; Yorkey, 1977) insist that the Qur'an is the overriding influence on written Arabic. Reference to the fact that written Arabic is considered to be the direct written word of Allah appears in nearly all analyses of Arabic rhetoric. Ostler (1987) even claims that because of the importance of Classical Arabic, speakers of Arabic do not look for great precision in meaning in writing. Since reading anything from Classical Arabic automatically means reading some words whose meanings have changed or have been lost for a 20th century audience, it is said that Arabic readers are not upset at reading texts whose meanings are not completely transparent.

Speakers of Arabic are proud of the neatness, flexibility, and logic of Classical Arabic grammar. It is a grammar that is highly systematic and unusually complex. Even the vocabulary is systematically built on permutations of three-letter roots. Arabic scholars characterize Classical Arabic as full of flamboyant imagery with a richness which permits the user to say the same thing in a great variety of ways.

Nearly all commentators on Arabic prose style are quick to refer to the heavy reliance on coordinating structures typical of Arabic writing. While English seeks hierarchy and subordination of one idea to another, Arabic rhetoric requires coordination, parallelism, and balancing of ideas (Ostler, 1987; Yorkey, 1977; Kaplan, 1966). The reliance on coordination evident in the English writing of native speakers of Semitic languages clashes with the English sense that the ability to subordinate ideas indicates rhetorical maturity. While English requires spotlighting a main idea and showing how other ideas relate to that main idea, Arabic rhetoric encourages the ability to find another way to say the same thing, and the Arabic language is rich enough to permit a skillful user to succeed in constructing complex parallels of ideas. Unfortunately, an English-speaking reader may take this planned coordination as simple repetition. The Arabic word for "and" is "wa" and it is said that English teachers at the University of Beirut, when Beirut was still a city, jokingly referred to the wa-wa method of organizing writing (Yorkey, 1977).

When the repetition expected in Arabic writing and the vigor and flamboyance available in the Arabic language are employed as strategies in English, the writing can look exaggerated and excessively assertive. And, in fact, at least one study of U.S. and Lebanese college students (Prothro, 1955) addresses the question of exaggeration in prose. In this study, statements which struck the English speakers as neutral were read as understatements by the Arabic speakers, and what was taken to be exaggeration by the English speakers struck the Arabic speakers as neutral.

The very respect that speakers of Arabic have for their language may cause unexpected problems for them in writing classes in the United States. Grabe and Kaplan (1989, 270) claim that speakers of Arabic focus more on form than on meaning when they write. Ostler (1987) asserts that because of this focus on beauty and balance rather than content and because of their respect for the writing of Classical Arabic and the Qur'an, Arabic students may have an especially difficult time using writing as a heuristic. They may feel uncomfortable writing formlessly and may be reluctant to simply write down anything that comes into their heads.

Hebrew, like Arabic, is a Semitic language but has undergone a different history and, therefore, presents a different picture from the point of view of English. Zellermayer's (1988) analysis of Hebrew writing causes her to conclude that Hebrew prose is more context-dependent than English and assumes much greater involvement on the part of the reader to interpret texts. Unlike English, Hebrew would then fall into Hinds's category of reader-responsible language, in which the reader is expected, and expects, to infer meaning from indirect or inexplicit writing.

European

Surprisingly little cross-cultural analysis of European languages has appeared in the literature on contrastive rhetoric. French school children are taught the tripartite text structure of *these-antithese-*

synthese, and there is some evidence that they carry this pattern over to English (Bassetti, 1990). German mathematics texts are said to resemble English, but German chemistry texts are characterized by a freedom to digress which would be unusual in English (Clyne, 1984).

The most closely analyzed of European languages has been Spanish rhetorical style. As with chemistry texts in German, in Spanish, and perhaps Slavic rhetoric, digressions and asides are attempts to link the point under discussion to other issues and as such are considered the hallmarks of intelligent writing. To show the breadth of their knowledge, writers are encouraged to explore each subtopic within a main topic at some length. The relative baldness characteristic of English writing may suggest to a Spanish-speaking reader a lack of range on the part of the writer, perhaps even intellectual narrow-mindedness.

Other differences have been detected. In English, as in Chinese, writers are encouraged to rely on specific and concrete examples or data. In Spanish it seems that the ability to generalize is favored and nurtured, the ability to see through scattered examples and data to underlying patterns linking them. Since the writer's job is to generalize from data, a reader's demand for the concrete data rather than the generalization may be viewed as the reader's unwillingness to believe or inability to follow the thrust of the generalization, revealing the reader's own inadequacies or, alternatively, challenging the writer's intelligence or knowledge.

Elegant Spanish writing is also said to require embellishments in order to conceal the organizational skeleton of the writing. For this reason, according to Spanish rhetoricians, Spanish writers are reluctant to use a technique as simple as enumeration without including what appear to English readers as irrelevant elaborations on each of the enumerated items (Collado, 1981).

Finally, Spanish writing achieves a leisurely elegance through lengthy introductions. In an essay written for an English writing placement exam, a newly arrived student from Spain addressed the question of whether animals should be used in experiments testing new products and drugs. The essay was about 250 words long. Here is the beginning:

> When life began on earth long time ago, that primitive life could seem nothing, just little celules lost in a great ocean. But these first forms of living were doing every time better. From little animals or plants to more sofisticated forms. And we see today, after millions of years of evolution that species that once were kings of their land now have dissapeared. Because they did other animals could survive. (*Unedited*)

The student continued in this way, musing on how old ideas in science give way to new ideas and about how quickly science is moving forward. At word 167 he wrote "So I agree with using . . . or even killing animals where those deaths are going to do better our lifes." The introduction took up over 150 of the 250-word total and began with the emergence of life on earth.

Conclusion

Because they have learned different rhetorical conventions and because they may not yet have developed a sense of their U.S. audience's requirements, ESL writers may produce writing which violates the expectations of native speakers of English. Some of their difficulties may be developmental, stemming from lack of experience in writing; others may result from simple lack of experience with English. Less proficiency in English means fewer options to choose from. But the difficulty may also stem from conflicting rhetorical conventions. Yet teachers obviously cannot be expected to be familiar with all the possible ways human beings have devised for thinking on paper. Since ESL students are trying to learn English patterns, what difference does it make what their culture's preferred styles are?

The insights into the rhetorics of other cultures that emerge from a study of contrastive rhetoric can be useful to both teachers and students. It should be helpful to teachers to know that particular options ESL students choose in their writing are not random but may come as a result of rhetorical constraints not shared by English speakers. Contrastive rhetoric studies show us a variety of ways to develop ideas in writing. The examples here from English, Chinese, Japanese, Arabic, and Spanish show us rhetorical styles which value such features as suggestiveness, precision, conciseness, leisureliness, effusiveness, or traditional patterns of organization. Thus, insight into the rhetorical patterns of our own and other cultures may help us avoid stereotypes caused by failing to recognize different culturally preferred writing styles and help us remain aware that all these systems are conventions.

Since the students themselves are probably unaware of the rhetorical constraints affecting their writing, some conscious knowledge of contrastive rhetoric may help them as well. In-class discussions in which ESL students are asked to reflect on some of the requirements of their own rhetorical traditions not only endorse the validity of their traditions but, when carried out in the presence of native students, may broaden the native students' awareness of, respect for, and curiosity about traditions in other countries, and thus work against the insularity of perspective from which some native students suffer.

Awareness of contrastive patterns does not necessarily produce improved writing (Schlumberger and Manglesdorf, 1989), but it does allow students to view certain writing problems they may have as evidence not so much of individual inadequacies as of their participation in other discourse communities besides those of their current environment. They come from other rhetorical traditions, which must be preserved, of course, but which cannot be applied wholesale to English writing. No matter what the language, writers still make choices indicating relationships of ideas, through repetition, parallel structure, choices of subordination and coordination, or relational words. By realizing that they are influenced by cultural preferences, these students become aware that long introductions, digressions, lack of directness, heavy use of coordination, or the opposite, are choices that they make as writers. Recognizing that writing is a matter of making such choices is a valuable insight for young writers.

What of the problem of imposing our English preferences on ESL students? They have their own rhetorical traditions; shouldn't we respect them? These students advance or are impeded in their progress by their ability to manipulate the target culture's symbol system, including its rhetoric. Research in reading shows that readers understand and recall better what they are familiar with and expect, and that applies both to content and to form, that is, to patterns of rhetorical development (Carrell, 1984; Connor, 1984, Connor and McCagg, 1983). This means that ESL students' texts are easier for their professors to read if the writers know their readers' rhetorical expectations and provide for them. Thus, it seems clear that writing teachers do have a responsibility to teach the expectations of the English audience to L2 writers and thereby to help them increase the perceived quality of their texts.

It is important, however, to try to keep in mind what it means to be asked to choose a way of expressing oneself that is foreign. Fan Shen's (1989) poignant testimony (see Chapter 6) reminds us of the painful process of trying to accommodate the requirements of both English and Chinese. Encouraged to express himself, to find his voice, to be himself in his writing, Shen realized how much his self, his voice, was Chinese, not English, and that the only way to fulfill the English requirement to be himself was to *not* be himself, to create a different English self that would be able to speak directly and explicitly. His real self, his Chinese self, could not.

Clearly, when dealing with students whose languages we do not share, we must remember how strong the link is between identity and language and remain sensitive to the difficult and sometimes painful juggling acts we may innocently be asking our students to perform.

Chapter Nine

Sentence-Level Errors

Problems at the discourse level are often fairly subtle, leaving the reader with the feeling that something is not quite right with a text but with no clear picture of where the problem lies. At the sentence level, however, errors are relatively obvious.

In the past, language teachers, including ESL teachers, influenced by behaviorist ideas about learning, considered language learning simply a matter of developing habits. Since language learners already had L1 habits, those habits were likely to be transferred directly into the L2 and therefore to interfere with the development of the new habits of the L2. With this view of language, it was obviously essential for teachers to help students avoid forming bad habits, and so language teachers were very concerned about preventing or eliminating all errors in a student's use of the L2.

The current prevailing view on errors among ESL teachers is similar to the view on errors among many L1 writing teachers. That is, ESL teachers are not particularly focused on errors, which are no longer regarded as evidence of students' failure to learn. Rather, errors are thought of as a natural part of the L2 learning process. At lower levels of proficiency, it is thought that as students are exposed to more of the L2 and acquire more of it, many of the errors they produce will naturally disappear. At the advanced level of ESL students in college classes, some ESL writing teachers have turned enthusiastically toward the non-error-based focus of the process approach to teaching writing. Two factors support this turn away from a concern with errors.

First, both research and some anecdotal evidence indicate that non-English-teaching faculty members are able to overlook errors made by ESL students (Santos, 1988; Leki, 1991b) (a generosity probably not extended as readily to native writers), especially if they are local errors, that is, errors which do not interfere with comprehension, as opposed to global errors, which do interfere (Burt and Kiparsky, 1972). In Santos's study, content-area faculty were clearly able to distinguish between the content and the form of the ESL writing and to evaluate the content separately.

Santos does note, however, that ESL errors caused irritation for the content-area faculty. Interestingly, perhaps predictably, two of the errors which the faculty found the most irritating and least acceptable, the double negative and subject/verb agreement, are likely to be produced by native speakers as well (Santos, 1988).[1]

On the other hand, although a typical ESL error like article usage, which is a local error, would rarely interfere with comprehension of the message, faculty may become irritated at errors in article usage simply because they are unaware that article usage is an extremely complex area of English usage. If it is achieved at all, mastery of the English article system by non-native speakers requires many years of contact with English. Presumably, the faculty mistakenly assumes that all these kinds of errors are careless errors of proofreading rather than language-learning errors (although article errors are almost certainly language-learning errors), and therefore, the faculty feels justified in blaming students for making them (Kroll, 1991). Unfortunately, instructions to proofread carefully may be *entirely* useless since ESL students may simply not recognize certain structures as errors. They may well have proofread to the best of their abilities but their abilities are not those of native speakers; they have an internalized sense of the language, an interlanguage version of English, which differs to varying degrees from that of native speakers. (See discussion of interlanguage later in this chapter.) From reading a text produced by an ESL writer, teachers have no way of knowing how much the student may have struggled to produce that form, perhaps writing and rewriting, not knowing exactly which form might be correct. This kind of struggle appears to occur especially with choice of vocabulary (Raimes, 1985; Arndt, 1987).

Whether errors are actually careless errors or language-learning errors cannot always be determined on the basis of the errors themselves. Unfortunately, what also remains undetermined is the extent to which people in the real world (e.g., potential employers of ESL students, particularly immigrant students) can tolerate or overlook writing errors, developmental or not. Nevertheless, it does appear that many faculty are able to overlook a certain number of ESL student writing errors.

The second factor influencing ESL writing teachers' turn away from a focus on errors in writing is the mass of evidence that both

[handwritten margin notes: error correction has little effect in error reduction]

grammar classes and error correction seem to have very little effect on students' ability to reduce the number of errors in their writing (See Leki, 1990a, for a summary of research on this issue.) The possible reasons for this failure to influence student writing by giving feedback on errors are many: the input or feedback may not be taken in by the student; the input may be confusing; the student may have too many other competing cognitive demands while writing; the student's level of language development may not be sufficiently advanced to receive the new information; the amount of correction necessary may be overwhelming. Furthermore, many of the most problematic, meaning-disturbing errors of ESL writers cannot be easily described, explained, and edited away.

[handwritten margin note: little agreement on which errors influence meaning]

A reasonable response to errors would seem to be to correct or point out errors which disturb meaning. But Davies (1985) explores the problems teachers face in attempting to determine which errors affect comprehensibility. First, what is incomprehensible for one reader may be perfectly comprehensible for another who may be accustomed to seeing that particular error and know how to interpret the grammatically flawed statement. Second, whether or not a grammatically flawed statement is comprehensible also depends heavily on the context in which the error is made. This means that each error must be treated as a separate and independent problem; error *types* cannot be categorized as more or less disturbing to comprehension. If this is the case, Davies suggests that teachers and students face the formidable task of addressing each error individually rather than being able to address whole categories of errors. This analysis may help to explain why grammar lessons, which do address whole categories of language forms, have so little effect on reducing the numbers of errors learners produce.

The task of assiduously addressing all errors in students' writing is simply too daunting. Furthermore, the content-area faculty surveyed in Santos's research (1988) could overlook grammatical errors, but they were disturbed by what they perceived as lack of maturity of thought and of rhetorical style in ESL students' writing—a problem, of course, not addressed by response to surface error. Thus, whatever the reason, teachers are increasingly reluctant to spend time marking errors if that activity seems to do the student so little good.

On the other hand, some ESL studies have shown a decrease in the number of errors students make after treatment—that is, after teacher feedback and/or explanation of their errors (Cohen and Cavalcanti, 1990; Fathman and Whalley, 1990).[2] Also, while advanced ESL students are less preoccupied with error than, for example, inexperienced native writers (Raimes, 1985), they may also expect and desire teacher correction of *all* their writing errors, maintaining that indications of errors do help their writing improve (Leki, 1991b; Radecki and Swales, 1988). These students may even see a teacher's reluctance to bother with errors as shirking duties. Furthermore, despite the influence of the process approach to teaching writing and its de-emphasis of error, many ESL writing teachers continue to feel the need to give feedback on language as well as on content and to focus students' attention on the divergence between their use and the standard use of the language. Finally, increasing numbers of ESL writing teachers are pointing out that error correction is not automatically inconsistent with a communicative or process approach to teaching writing. Whether or not it is inconsistent depends on when and how the errors are addressed. Addressing errors toward the end of a writing task and in a non-punitive manner is not likely to block an ESL writer's ability to generate and develop ideas. (See Chapter 3 for a discussion of ESL and basic writing students' divergent attitudes toward written error.)

Sources of Error

ESL students make many sentence-level errors; many ESL students desire and expect correction of their errors. For teachers who intend to take on this task, it might help to know the source of some of these errors. This information may clarify how far we can expect to get in helping students to produce more normal English formations.

As in the case of larger rhetorical patterns, language researchers have gradually changed their analysis of the sources of sentence-level errors. First the students' L1 was blamed (interference or language transfer errors); then it seemed that the nature of English itself created inevitable learner error; and more recently error has been thought of in terms of learning and production strategies.

When language learning was thought of in terms of habit-building, researchers hoped to be able to predict what kinds of L2 structures would give learners trouble based on the differences between L1 and L2. Linguists would do a contrastive analysis of the two languages to see where they were similar and where they were different. It was thought that the more different two structures were in two languages, the more difficulty students would have in learning the new structures. Furthermore, it was assumed that the habits of the L1 would interfere with the students' learning of the L2.

What researchers found was that contrastive analysis was not very effective in predicting the errors learners would make based on their L1. They found that the number of interference or transfer errors was quite small. Burt (1975) cites a study of 193 errors in English of German learners: only 25 percent of lexical errors, only 10 percent of syntax errors, and no morpheme errors could have been caused by L1 transfer. Furthermore, it became clear that the structures which were most different between two languages did not necessarily cause the most trouble; instead, structures that were fairly similar but used in slightly different circumstances were often the ones most difficult for learners to master.

Out of these discoveries arose error analysis. This time linguists did not try to predict the errors learners would make, but instead examined the errors they actually made to determine which structures gave which learners the most difficulty. The problem with this approach surfaced when certain contradictions became apparent. Schachter (1974) reported on a study of Middle Eastern and Asian learners of English and noted that Middle Eastern students made more errors in constructing adjective clauses than did Asian students. Yet Arabic and Farsi construct adjective clauses almost the same way English does, with the exception that in Arabic and Farsi, the relative (adjective) clause marker is used in addition to, not in place of, the pronoun it refers to. Speakers of Arabic or Farsi, for example, often produce this kind of error: *I finally found the book which I had been looking for it.*[3]

What Schachter found, however, was that the reason Asian students were producing far fewer errors in adjective clauses was that they were avoiding using those clauses, whose structures differed so much from the structures of Chinese or Japanese. In other words, by simply counting the number of errors learners made in using a structure, error analysis was still not giving an accurate picture of the difficulty of that structure for learners. Middle Eastern students had no trouble using adjective clauses but made mistakes, while Asian students made no mistakes because they had so much difficulty using adjective clauses that they avoided them whenever possible.

In all these views of error, learners seem passive, almost victimized by their L1, which makes unexpected and unwanted intrusions on the L2 learning process. Yet studies also reveal a different picture of L1 interference or transfer, one in which the learner is making active decisions about which structures to transfer. A study of Dutch students (cited in Krashen and Terrell, 1983) showed that they were more likely to transfer L1 forms which are unmarked (that is, the usual or neutral way to say something), taking a chance that the structure might be the same in L2, than marked forms (unusual, perhaps metaphorical uses of the language), which they thought might be peculiar only to their L1. They thought, for example, that *break a leg* is more likely to be correct in English

If meaning/sound its structure/to me, I, student, I put it might/this wrong/ will even its not

than *waves breaking on the shore* even though both appear in both Dutch and English. The same constraints applied to syntax. Both Dutch and English have the expression *The book reads well*. When asked to judge whether that expression in English was probably correct or not, the Dutch subjects judged it to be probably incorrect in English. It is a marked form (that is, not the usual way to use *read*) and therefore, they reasoned, probably language specific, a direct translation from Dutch. In making such judgments, the learner is not a passive victim of the features of L1 but is actively making guesses about the nature of L2. Findings such as these force a reassessment of the influence of L1 on L2, casting doubt on the overriding role that learners' L1s were thought to play in L2 learning and acquisition.

It does seem clear that students' first languages have an influence on the kinds of problems they will have with English.[4] (See Swan and Smith, 1988, for fascinating comparisons between the structure of English and some twenty other languages.) But although a small number of errors in English can be associated with particular L1 backgrounds, as the Burt (1975) study showed, the vast majority of errors made by learners of English resemble each other and, therefore, seem to be a result of the structure of English itself regardless of the L1. Furthermore, as morpheme acquisition studies have shown, early stages of L1, of L2, of simplified registers like baby talk or foreigner talk, and of pidgins all seem to show about the same morpheme acquisition order for English. In other words, if English is the target language, a similar pathway is followed to get there by all learners regardless of where they are coming from linguistically. Why might this be the case? Linguists suggest that morpheme acquisition studies point to the existence of a universal grammar which all humans rely upon in taking in a new language.

Universal grammar

Thus, in the 1970s a different perspective on errors emerged. Errors began to be thought of as evidence of a learner's interlanguage configuration. Interlanguage is a succession of the learners' mental depictions of the grammar of the new language and is thought to have a structure of its own, distinct from both the L1 and the L2 (Selinker, 1972). In other words, interlanguage is not a hybrid of two other languages, but the result of learners' active attempts to process and use data from L2 language input to build their interlanguage. When learners make grammatical mistakes, it is thought that these mistakes are images of learners' interlanguage. Linguists would like to be able to describe the structure of interlanguages, but this task is impossible since interlanguages are not stable and continually shift with new language input.

The learners' attempts at language-processing language of sorts own language they change as learner learns more own version of the L2

In the past, then, grammar errors were thought of as first language interference of some kind in the L2. In the current view, however, errors are seen as evidence of a variety of language learning and language production strategies. In an apparently automatic effort to reduce cognitive load, for example, learners create their own version of the L2 as best they can by simplifying the L2 input, taking in and registering essential features of the L2 input but temporarily ignoring some of the details in order to remember and analyze those main features. Learners also overgeneralize in their unconscious analysis of L2 structures; for example, if the learner already has in place a version of English which assigns -s to third person singular forms, the learner may at first overgeneralize that rule by adding -s to modal auxiliaries as well, producing forms like *She cans do it. Such forms are clearly rule governed and evidence of the learner's active efforts to take in and analyze the structure of the L2.

Transfer of first language forms is also no longer considered interference of the first language in the second language but rather a learning/communication strategy of falling back on the first language when the necessary second language forms are not present in the learner's interlanguage. In other words, if a learner needs to produce a form which does not exist in that learner's interlanguage version of L2 (that is, if the learner wants to say something in English and doesn't yet know how to say it in English), the learner scans the L1 for forms that will accomplish the same communicative task and uses the L1 forms to replace the missing L2 forms. Thus, L1 transfer can be positive, when a structure is the same in L1 and L2, or negative, when the structures are different and, therefore, the student's gamble does not succeed.

This notion of both positive and negative transfer helps explain why certain L1s facilitate the acquisition of an L2. If the two languages are linguistically close, the learner's gambles are likely to succeed often. Furthermore, the more languages an individual knows, the more already acquired structures the learner can fall back on, which explains why people who learn a second language typically find that learning a third or a fourth is much easier than learning the second one was.

The feature of interlanguage which prevents a full linguistic description is its instability. A learner's progress is not stable and steady but is characterized by movements backwards and forwards along the path toward the L2, as new input, previously too complex to take in, is analyzed and processed. This analyzing and processing causes previously in-place interlanguage features to shift. Sometimes, under certain conditions, a seemingly acquired correct L2 form is dropped in favor of an error. The learner is then sometimes said to have hit a linguistic ceiling. This phenomenon occurs in a variety of situations: if the learner must suddenly deal with new or difficult subject matter in the L2; experiences anxiety; lacks practice in the L2, even for a short while; or slackens attention, including while relaxing. Sometimes interlanguage pronunciation, that is, mispronunciation, is induced simply by using L1 words or even proper names in L2 production. In other words, although a student's L2 language facility may be at a certain level, a number of different circumstances can trigger a reversion to interlanguage forms which had apparently ceased to exist. Such reversion can certainly appear in a student's writing as well, under both stressful and relaxed conditions—for example, while under the stress of writing an essay exam or while relaxed and using free writing as a heuristic.

Normally, as language learners continue receiving input from the target language, their interlanguage reshapes itself in increasing conformity to the L2. For reasons not completely understood, however, certain interlanguage forms become fixed, or fossilized, and no amount of input seems to be able to induce a re-analysis of the fossilized form to put it more in line with the L2. Fossilization manifests itself most frequently and obviously in "foreign" accents but may occur in any form of the target language. Fossilized interlanguage forms are particularly difficult to alter, possibly because the learner is for whatever reason unmotivated to identify completely with the target discourse community.

Types of Errors

Although non-ESL writing teachers are often skilled grammarians, they find the errors advanced ESL students make in their writing unfamiliar and sometimes feel at a loss about how to deal with them. Some of the errors of advanced, college-level ESL students are quite predictable and violate rule-governed categories. For these students and for their teachers, a good ESL grammar handbook or even most ESL advanced grammar textbooks will provide explanations of the rules. Unfortunately for the students, however, many errors are mis-selections of features of arbitrary categories of English grammar or violate rules so complex that it almost seems necessary to be a native speaker in order just to understand the rule, let alone apply it. (See the section below on prepositions, for example.)

The following are some of the typical ESL errors likely to appear in the writing of advanced ESL students.

Countable/Uncountable Nouns and Corresponding Quantity Terms

English common nouns are more or less divided between countable nouns (like *books, tables,* or *ideas*) and uncountable nouns (like *work, help,* or *importance*). Most advanced ESL students have little trouble remembering which quantity terms go with countable nouns (*many, few, a few*) and which go with uncountable nouns (*much, little, a little*). A series of learnable rules govern each of the categories. The trick is identifying which nouns are countable and which are not. *Problem* is countable; *trouble* is usually not. *Assignment* is countable; *homework* is not. *Suggestion* is countable; *advice* is not. And so on. Usages like **many informations, *an advice,* and **a news* are probably all the result of mis-identifying the noun.

There are also complicating exceptions: nouns which can be both countable or uncountable and, to make matters worse, change in meaning: *to have company* versus *to have a company.* Other words are murky: *people* looks singular but takes a plural verb; the same is true for *cattle* (the cattle are), but not necessarily *faculty, group, class,* or *committee* (the committee is), which also differ from *police* (the police are).

Adjectives Acting as Nouns

English uses certain descriptive adjectives as nouns—*the young, the old, the strong*—but many students will, logically, want to treat them fully as nouns and make them plural: **the youngs, *the olds, *the strongs.* Other adjectives would not be used as nouns at all: **the responsible(s).*

Articles

The biggest problem with the indefinite article (*a* or *an*) or the indefinite plural noun without an article (*books, tables*) is related to whether the noun is countable or not. Once that determination is made, most problems related to the indefinite article are eliminated. The indefinite article is not normally used with uncountable nouns, which also do not usually have plural forms (**an advice, *advices*).

The rules for the use of the definite article are much more complicated and difficult to grasp. Rules govern many of the uses of *the,* but decisions about article usage must be made for every noun, making errors difficult to avoid. Typical problems for many European language speakers include:

- Use of *the* with certain abstract nouns: not *We must protect the nature*, but *We must protect the environment.*

- Use of *the* with abstract nouns which are not post-modified: not *The life is not easy*, but *The life of a single parent is not easy.*

Speakers of Polish, Persian, dialects of the Indian subcontinent, and many other languages fail to recognize the need for some determiner before singular countable nouns:

- *In traditional Indian family, house where family lives belongs to man of family.*

- *Government of Iran was corrupt under Shah.*

- *We are angry because price of bread goes up every day.*

or with quantity terms:

- *Some of class was unable to attend.*

Agreement of Noun Determiners

Probably because of the way they are pronouncing the words, some students (especially Spanish speakers) fail to make the agreement between a noun and its demonstrative modifier: *this doctors.* Many students also forget to make numbers and the nouns they modify agree — *seven page* — or mistakenly create agreement between numbers and nouns acting as adjectives: *A five-dollars bill* or *three five-dollars bills.* And Romance language speakers tend to make modifying adjectives agree with plural nouns: *the beautifuls mornings.*

Progressive Verb Forms

The distinction between progressive or continuous tenses and simple tenses creates problems because the students misinterpret the meaning of the tense in a given situation:

- *I am reading the newspaper every day.*

- *Now we read Shakespeare in the literature class.*

The adverbial expression *every day* does not usually co-occur with the progressive or continuous verb form, which may suggest action in progress at the moment of speaking, while the adverb *now* does typically co-occur with the progressive.

Learners also forget that a subcategory of English verbs tends to be used primarily in the simple, non-continuous form even under conditions which would normally call for continuous forms:

- *What are you wanting?*
- *I am owning a small car.*

Present Perfect Verb Forms

English uses present perfect to describe action or a situation that may have begun in the past but continues to be true in the present: *I have been here for six months now.* Many other languages use the present tense in these cases, and students may therefore produce: *I am here for six months now.* A form that looks like the English present perfect exists in many European languages, but it is not always used the same way: *I have seen him yesterday* does not work in English but would work in French or German, for example.

Modal Auxiliaries

There are certain rule-governed formal features of modal auxiliary usage which are fairly easy to learn and, if the writers are attending to form, easy to employ: modals do not agree in number with the subject (*He cans do it*) and modals are followed by simple, not finite verb forms (*He can does it*). The problem does not lie here but in the complex, subtle meanings expressed by these auxiliaries in all their forms, meanings very difficult for ESL students to acquire and use comfortably.

Consider the confusion created by the meaning of the modals in the following sentences:

- *In Zaire students must stand when the teacher enters.*
- But: *In France they must not stand when the teacher enters.*
- Versus: *In France they don't have to stand when the teacher enters.*

Must not and *don't have to* have entirely different meanings, making it difficult for students to decide how to negate the necessity expressed by *must.*

Another example of the different meaning of modals is demonstrated in the following sentences:

- *You could have helped.* (Meaning: *You didn't.*)
- *She couldn't have passed that test.* (Meaning either: *I think she didn't* or *I'm surprised she did.*)

Passive/Active Voice

Although students occasionally have difficulty with the long and complicated verb phrases sometimes needed to express passive voice, again the problem does not lie so much in the rule-governed and learnable forms, or in the meaning of the passive generally, as in the categorization of certain verbs.

Intransitive verbs, for example, are never passive:

- *A real revolution was occurred with her election to office.*
- *Such events had never been happened before.*

Unlike most verbs, which take animate subjects in the active voice (*I am enjoying this class; I want that book*), "psychologically reversed" verbs (Burt and Kiparsky, 1972) typically take animate subjects in the passive voice. Students overgeneralize the usual pattern to cover the psychologically reversed verbs and produce:

- *I am quite interesting in this matter*, instead of *I am interested in this matter.*
- *That class is so long I always bore in it*, instead of *I am always bored in it.*

Still other frequently misused active/passive forms fit no special category: *Vietnam locates in Southeast Asia.*

Sequence of Tenses

The rules for appropriate sequence of tenses in English are somewhat complicated but fairly straightforward, systematic, and therefore learnable.

For students whose languages do not show time changes by morphological changes in the verb — Asian languages, for example — it takes quite a while to sense (or acquire) the difference in meaning which native speakers feel when the verb tense switches from, for example, past to present. Since those tense changes have only thin psychological reality for these students, they may have a difficult time remembering to stay with the same tense. Typically, unless they are concentrating on tenses, these students will tend to revert to a kind of time-neutral present tense. Such errors are not usually caused by misunderstanding the rules of tense sequencing but rather lapses in focus in editing.

Verb Forms

Learners often use simple verb forms where gerunds are required (after prepositions, as subjects of sentences):

- *By stop the destruction of the Amazon Valley, we can slow down global warming.*
- *Cut down more trees creates hotter conditions.*
- *We need forests for increase the world's oxygen.*

Verb Complements

Verb complementation is one of the most difficult aspects of English syntax to master because complementation depends entirely on arbitrary subcategories of verbs, each of which takes one or more types of complementation but not others. The following sentences exemplify the types of errors in complementation typical of the writing of ESL students:

- *The ministers recommended the president to explore peace talks with the guerrillas. (The ministers implored the president to explore . . . .)
- *They wanted that the new policy would begin immediately. (They expected that the new policy would begin immediately.)
- *I wish I will get a good grade in this course. (I hope I will get a good grade in this course.)
- *This compromise succeeded to bring about a ceasefire. (This compromise was expected to bring about a ceasefire.)
- *They stopped to negotiate. (They refused to negotiate.)
- *The rebels risk to fight for the freedom of their country. (The rebels continue to fight for . . . or The rebels continue fighting for . . . .
- *The lawyer requested for a postponement. (The lawyer asked for a postponement.)

The large number of examples is intended to suggest the variety of ways complementation takes place in English. Unfortunately for ESL students, the main verb gives no hint whatsoever which complement it requires, and students must either acquire or memorize which verbs take which complements.

Adjective Clauses

Aside from the usual problem of deciding whether an adjective clause is restrictive or non-restrictive, most of the problems ESL students have with adjective clauses fall into the following categories:

- Asian language students omit obligatory clause markers: *The car hit the post had crossed the traffic barrier.
- Persian, Arabic, and related language students fail to eliminate the pronoun which the clause marker replaces in English: *The biggest problem (that) we have to face it continues to be the war.
- Reductions of adjective clauses to participial phrases cause problems in deciding whether to use a present or a past parti-

cipial phrase. (*Worked all day, the committee finally came to an agreement./*Frying in oil, chruschikis have a lot of calories.) Even the terms present and past participial phrases create confusion since they imply present and past times or tenses instead of merely forms.

Adverb Clauses

Students from several different language backgrounds make mistakes in constructing adverbial clauses:

- *Although international students often need money, but they are not usually allowed to work while in the United States.
- *Because of their visa does not permit work off campus, they can only get jobs that pay little money.
- *Some students are too poor that they can hardly have enough to eat.

Noun Clauses and Reported Speech

The rules for noun clauses and reported speech are learnable; however, students often make mistakes with these structures, possibly from inattention or cognitive overload since these structures require attention to several linguistic details:

- *I was not aware of that I had to register early.
- *The committee wanted to know why did he do it.
- *They asked that what was happening.

Non-referential Pronoun Subjects

Students confuse and misuse it and there when they are used merely to hold the subject place. For example:

- *After the game, it was a big party in the streets.
- *We are five from Germany on the team. (There are five of us on the team from Germany.)

The use of there in this type of sentence is not easy for students to grasp or for teachers to explain. This use of there indicates to the listener/reader that the speaker/writer intends to make a comment about something whose existence the listener/reader is assumed to be unaware of.

The use of non-referential it is easier to grasp but hard to remember for many students whose languages do not always require an explicit subject, such as Spanish or Russian:

- *Was a beautiful day!
- *In spite of the difficult subject matter, is no problem for me to understand chemistry textbooks.

Fragments and Run-on Sentences

Rules of punctuation vary widely across languages. In Spanish, for example, commas are required to join series of related thoughts where English requires periods. In some languages, exact rules for punctuation do not exist or are not agreed upon, making some students' use of marks of punctuation seem almost arbitrary. Students are also confused by the different punctuation required in association with connective words with more or less the same meanings, such as but, however, and although, each requiring different punctuation. Typical errors are:

- *Students are required to take some English courses; although, they may not want to.
- *Most students survive their experience abroad, however they have many adjustments to make.

Prepositions

Most of the errors discussed above can be addressed by consciously learning rules about the operation of English grammar even though those rules may be complex. Much more frustrating are the many errors for which no rules apply, where usage is idiomatic and must be learned on a case-by-case basis. Most notorious are English prepositions. While some prepositions like up or down refer to a physical reality which students can draw upon in making decisions about which preposition to use, no logic or external reality guides the selection of prepositions which appear in association with other words:

- To talk about versus *to mention about or *to discuss about.
- To be in need of (need as a noun) versus *to need of (need as a verb).

There are countless numbers more of these collocations. Also following no discernible system are the many phrasal or two-(or more) word verbs, each with wildly different, highly idiomatic meanings in spite of their being based on the same verb. Consider:

- To put on (clothes) versus to put off (an engagement — not the opposite of to put on) versus to put out (a fire).

- *To make up*, which can mean to put make-up on, to become reconciled, to invent, or to complete something previously missed, like an exam.
- *To get over, to get up, to get away,* or *to get by.*

The lists go on. Unfortunately for ESL students, phrasal verbs are extremely common. They are used more often in speech than their higher-register counterparts, which at least speakers of European languages might be more likely to recognize. Because the corresponding higher-register words often have Latinate roots, it is not surprising, for example, for Romance language speakers to know the meaning of *extinguish* but not of *put out.* Native speakers ironically make the mistake of trying to simplify their speech to non-natives by using "easier," that is, lower-register lexical items which the non-natives are in fact *less* likely to recognize than more sophisticated terms. It is also students' misuse of prepositions or phrasal verbs like these that many non-ESL faculty focus on when they complain about ESL errors. Perhaps they throw up their hands in despair at these problems precisely because they themselves see no systematic way of addressing them and because misuse of these parts of English so easily causes miscommunication.

Conclusion

Initially, and unfortunately, sentence-level errors may be the most salient feature of ESL student writing. In some cases, teachers fear the extra work they feel they will need to do to correct these students' errors, and for that reason, they may not feel enthusiastic about having an ESL student in class, particularly not in a class which requires a great deal of writing. In some cases, teachers may even associate many surface-level errors with lack of education or intelligence. Another fear sometimes expressed is that teachers will be forced to lower their standards for writing or use a double standard, one for native students and another, more lax standard for ESL students. Perhaps worst of all, in some schools and some classrooms, ESL students are simply ignored, receiving the "foreign student C" as a course grade for simply having appeared in class regularly.

These kinds of reactions are truly distressing and arise from misperceptions about language and language learning. It is important to remember that students learn a great deal that teachers do not teach and that exposure to English in communicative situations goes a long way toward providing students with language input which they automatically analyze and process as they reformulate their interlanguage or mental image of the grammar of English. It is also important to remember that these processes take time. The following chapter discusses other issues related to the question of responding to both the content and the form of ESL student writing.

Chapter Ten

Responding to ESL Writing

Much of the insight on responding to the writing of native speakers applies to the writing of ESL students as well. Most teachers already know a great deal about responding to student writing and about the kind of responses that fail.

Why Feedback Fails

Studies show that students have a tendency to reject or to ignore feedback on writing which they consider dead, that is, a final draft with a grade (Burkland and Grimm, 1986). We also know that even native speakers sometimes have trouble understanding written feedback on their writing for a variety of reasons. Sometimes the teacher's handwriting is hard to read. Sometimes students are not sure exactly which part of their text a comment is addressed to. Sometimes the gist of the comment itself is unclear; many teachers have had the experience of rereading comments they themselves have written on student texts and no longer being able to figure out what the comment was intended to get at. Sometimes the comment seems inapplicable to the student. For example, a request for clarification may make no sense to the writer if the text already seems clear to the writer. Students may respond to a request for an example for which they do not themselves perceive the need by mechanically adding material. The reader, usually the teacher, may then find that the additional material seems unrelated or does not clarify or exemplify the point the reader assumes the writer to be making.

Sometimes writers may both understand and perceive the need for a change in their texts and yet do not know how to go about making the change. All of these problems have surfaced in research on native-speaking writers; for non-natives these problems intensify.

Student writers, and experienced writers as well, sometimes reject certain kinds of response to the content of their writing. If Belenky's (1986) and Perry's (1981) descriptions of cognitive development are accurate, students who are at certain levels of development may feel that their ideas or their opinions must be accepted simply by virtue of being their opinions; that is, the students purposely want to make no broader claim for the validity of their opinions and feel they have a natural right to hold any opinions they want. These students may read teacher feedback requesting support for these opinions as the teachers' attempts to force students to agree with what the teachers believe or as the teachers' unwillingness to accept opinions which differ from their own. These students then may resent and/or resist responding to teacher commentary on the content of their writing.

An interesting study of ESL student responses to feedback (Radecki and Swales, 1988) showed that graduate students in particular resisted suggestions to alter content. They seemed to perceive the English teacher as a qualified expert on English grammar and usage but not qualified to comment on the content of their writing. For example, engineering or business administration graduate students would dismiss the English teacher's request for a clarification as unreasonable, insisting that clarification would be unnecessary for those in the same discipline, that anyone in that field would understand the student's point.

Finally, feedback on student writing also falls short of its goal when the changes suggested or requested in the feedback are too readily accepted by student writers. Sperling and Freedman's (1987) "good girl" assumed that any requests or suggestions her teacher made must be accommodated even when the young student author clearly did not understand why the teacher had made the comments. The "good girl" surrendered authority over her text immediately, assuming that the teacher always obviously knew better than she. Such behavior is also not uncommon among ESL students. While the graduate students in Radecki and Swales's (1988) study resisted teacher intervention in their writing, many others will unquestioningly alter both the form and the content of their writing, assuming, like the "good girl," that the native-speaking teacher must know what is required in English writing. This abdication of responsibility for their own texts means, at minimum, a failure to restructure perceptions and assumptions about good writing in English.

Goals for ESL Student Writing

That ESL students are different from native-speaking students becomes apparent in the reactions which their writing elicits in native-speaking readers and (as pointed out in the chapter on basic writers or second dialect students) in their goals and purposes for learning to write in English. ESL students claim that their content-area teachers are not particularly concerned with their grammatical accuracy (Leki, 1991b), that these teachers take for granted that ESL students will make errors. Thus, even though grammatical and mechanical errors may initially be the most salient feature of ESL student writing, content-area teachers may not penalize them for errors in their written English. On the other hand, ESL students themselves seem to be quite interested in grammatical accuracy (Leki, 1991b) and want English teachers to point out all their errors. They seem more eager to correct errors and less discouraged about making them than their native-speaking counterparts. This is not to say that when errors are pointed out to them, they are necessarily successful in correcting the errors, either in the short or the long run; some of their interest in having all errors marked may be earnest and unrealistic intention to profit from these markings, and usually to profit more than can possibly be accomplished, particularly if these students are behaving like the "good girl" and shifting responsibility for learning onto their teachers. Finally, outside the school context, for international students if not for immigrant ESL students, once many of these ESL students graduate and leave the United States, they may have little reason to write English at all. Thus, ESL students typically make more errors than native-speaking students, are more interested in dealing with them (*even though* they may not profit much from the corrections), are less penalized than native speakers for making errors, and may have less need to write error-free English after completing their education.

As teachers deal with ESL writing, then, the question arises, how good must the writing of these students become? What exactly do we want our students to be able to do in English? Their own varied goals aside for the moment, what should *our* goals for these students be? Can we have the same goals for ESL students as we may have for native-speaking writers? Should we, for example, or can we, expect that these ESL students will use *English* writing as a means of self-exploration, as a means of discovery and learning about themselves as we do expect from native students (Brannon and Knoblauch, 1982)? Is this a presumptuous goal for ESL graduate students, many of whom are highly sophisticated, even eminent professionals in their fields? Faigley (1989) asserts that in evaluating writing, teachers are "as much or more interested in *who* they want

their students to be as in *what* they want their students to write"
(396). If this is the case, then we must be particularly cautious
about using our sense of the importance of self-exploration and
discovery to impose an identity on ESL students which necessarily
reflects only our own notions of self and cannot take into account
the worlds these students come from.

The Politics of Teaching Writing

If a potential danger exists in asking ESL students to use writing to
broaden themselves as human beings, when their only intention
is to use English in the most utilitarian and pragmatic way, the
counterpoint to that danger may be evident in the position many
ESL teachers take in teaching writing, especially to pre-departure
international students or students in language institutes but not yet
matriculated into the university, therefore presumably not yet in a
position to know much about the target culture. That position is
that the ESL teacher's job is to present the forms of English (forms
of writing, speech, interacting with others, everything that the
students might have to do with language) as accurately as they can
and to direct students, not to adopt those norms (or to abandon
native norms), but to conform superficially to those norms when
dealing with the target culture. In many cases, it is precisely the
ESL teacher's revulsion at the idea of attempting to change the
student's values, and by extension to ask the student to abandon
the native norms, which results in a staunchly a-political refusal to
deal with the question of who the student is and what the confron-
tation between the student's culture and the target culture means
philosophically and politically. This position is similar to attitudes
sometimes directed toward second dialect native English-speaking
students: in order to succeed, to be empowered, these students are
told they must become bilingual and learn the privileged dialect of
the currently ruling class. Like second dialect students, the directive
ESL students may have heard most clearly may have been to conform
superficially to the norms of the target community, not to worry
about questioning those norms or thinking critically about them,
only to use them to the students' own advantage. In a sense the
assumption here is that the student has *the right* to come away from
the interaction with the target community unchanged.

However much we may resist the idea, our responses to the
writing of ESL students and our goals for them in our writing
courses are, in fact, laden with political content. If we ask our
students to reproduce standard written English and to organize
their thoughts along lines purportedly most familiar to native-

speaking readers, we are also "asking them to situate themselves within a particular socio-political context, and we respond to and judge their writing according to how accurately they are able to do so" (Land and Whitley, 1989, 289). This means that if they cannot accurately situate themselves where we expect them to be, they fail. And the failure is at least as much a political failure as a linguistic failure. They did not play the role we assigned them. Thus, the ominous reverse side of the writing teacher's job of helping to initiate writing students into the academic discourse community is the attempt to indoctrinate them into a particular worldview, and, for ESL students most notably, to colonize them.

Aside from the dramatic political consequences of teaching English and teaching writing, we should probably also keep in mind the special nature of school-sponsored writing, differing, as it appears to, from all other types of writing. Biber's (1988) multivariate analysis of hundreds of texts from a wide variety of writing contexts (for example, personal letters, professional letters, general fiction, science fiction, romantic fiction, editorials, press reports, press reviews, biographies, academic prose, official documents) reveals that student essays are a separate category unto themselves, unlike any other type of the published and unpublished English writing he examined. How can we justify teaching the conventions of this type of writing to ESL students (and to native students, for that matter) when it has no wider application? Can our goal possibly be limited to teaching ESL students how to write excellent student essays?

More pragmatically, should we work at style, at encouraging the use of complex sentence structures and broad and varied vocabulary? If we do address such concerns in our classes, how do we evaluate the performance of ESL students, who often must make enormous efforts just to express their ideas in English or to create prose free of jarring or distracting errors? Or should we be satisfied if ESL students manage only a prosaic, simple style (Brodkey, 1983)?

These are questions about our goals as teachers. More pertinent are the goals of the ESL students themselves. And unfortunately, more pertinent still may be the institutional goals fixed for all students graduating from particular institutions, which we, as well as the ESL students, have no choice but to accommodate until we can change them where necessary.

Effective Response Strategies

In the meantime, thanks to the great deal of thinking that has gone on among researchers and teachers of native speakers, we have some idea of what kinds of feedback on writing might be successful in accomplishing the goals of students, teachers, and institutions. Feedback on the writing of both natives and non-natives is generally more effective if it is given when the students have the opportunity to incorporate the comments into their writing rather than if it appears on a dead, final text.

Techniques developed to help native English-speaking students consciously focus on how their ideas are organized usually work for non-native speakers as well. One way for students to make visible to themselves the overall structure of their texts is to briefly describe the content of each paragraph of a piece of writing (in this paragraph I talk about this; in the next one about that). This simple procedure allows the students to get an entirely non-evaluative overview of how their texts are constructed.

Another potentially useful technique for analyzing smaller components of text in more detail is based on topical structure analysis (Connor and Farmer, 1990). In this procedure, students circle the topic of each independent clause in a paragraph (or text). This allows them to note the degree to which they bring up new subjects in a paragraph. After students analyze their texts in these ways, these overviews allow many of the structural features of their texts to stand out and may help them to see on their own any anomalies or unintended features. At this point, feedback can be helpful to indicate what a reader's expectations about the organization of the text might be.

Certainly, teachers can provide this type of feedback, looking over the paragraph descriptions or topical structure analyses with an eye toward strengthening or tightening an argument or an exposition. But as many writing teachers know, students are also quite adept at giving this type of feedback, and ESL students are no exception. Student readers can be asked, for example, to repeat the procedure referred to above in which the writer describes the contents of each paragraph of a piece of writing. If a writer discovers that the writer's notion of what each paragraph covers is different from the reader's analysis, the writer has a clear potential trouble spot to address.

Many writing teachers now use peer response or peer editing groups. Since international students are likely to be unfamiliar with peer responding, they will need guidance and practice to be able to respond helpfully. They may, in fact, need specific guidance in working in groups as well. Furthermore, peer responding cannot work exactly the same way with ESL students as it does with native English speaking students. (See Leki, 1990b, for a discussion of potential difficulties of using peer responding with ESL students.) However, with appropriate, specific questions to guide them and with practice, ESL students often become perceptive readers of their classmates' texts with regard to content and organization. (They are able to provide far less help to classmates with editing.)

As with native speakers, it makes sense to give feedback on content first. Once the content more or less expresses what the student was aiming for, feedback on accuracy aids editing of revised versions of a piece of writing. However, if students are misusing words, phrases, or structures that will clearly recur in or be essential to a particular piece of writing, there is no point in having them recopy incorrect versions of these features of English; it makes more sense to make *limited* interventions of these kinds earlier. In this way, students can incorporate these limited numbers of corrected words or forms into subsequent revisions.

Although sometimes ESL students are insistent about having errors corrected on every piece of writing they do (including final drafts) and may question the value of unmarked work (such as journals), evidence from L2 writing researchers suggests that even the most intensive, systematic attention to grammatical errors produces insignificant improvement in subsequent writing tasks (Robb, Ross, and Shortreed, 1986).

In most institutional settings, non-natives are required to make unreasonably great strides in their mastery of English in a given term. The temptation is great to try to help them by commenting on all aspects of their writing. Since ESL students make large numbers of sentence-level errors and may need special guidance with unfamiliar rhetorical patterns, commentary can easily become overwhelming. Students may benefit more from a more limited approach to feedback in which teachers address only some aspects of content and form in each paper. More importantly, ESL students need extra *time*, not only to write, revise, and edit individual pieces of writing but also to make global improvements in English.

Sometimes the teacher's or the institution's impatience for improvement is surpassed only by that of the students themselves. These students are not usually more informed about language acquisition or learning than anyone else (including institutions) and may have unreasonably high expectations, hoping, for example, to achieve error-free writing within a short period of time. They may become particularly frustrated if English teachers continue to point out problems in their writing while content-area teachers, not feeling obligated to give such help, do not. This is not necessarily to say that content-area faculty should attend to writing problems but that English teachers may need to be sensitive to the particular frustration of ESL students who are good students used to mastering subject matter easily and receiving top evaluations and who find that their progress in English is excruciatingly slow. Overwhelming quantities of feedback may inadvertently discourage these students even further, despite their calls to have all errors in their writing indicated.

Since there may be a tendency, especially among undergraduate international students, to accept teacher commentary without question, it becomes even more important that these students understand as fully as possible the need for changes a teacher might suggest. As far as possible, they must be helped to internalize the need for those changes, to put themselves in the reader's place to appreciate the basis for the suggestion. By the same token, and as with native students, it is important that ESL students understand the grammar or usage rule, if there is one, governing suggestions for sentence-level structural changes.

Leading students to those kinds of understandings may be more difficult to accomplish in written than in oral feedback, but oral feedback creates problems for ESL students to which native students may not be as susceptible. Since a great deal of cognitive energy may be required for some students to negotiate orally in an L2, less is left for remembering. Non-natives are not able to remember as much in English as they would in their native languages or as native speakers can. Students can read and reread written feedback but may find oral feedback slipping away from them even if they fully understand it at the time it is given. It is not a certainty either that they do understand even when they say they do since they may be reluctant to ask for repetition or clarification. Thus, while oral conferences are superior to written feedback in many respects, they must also be handled with particular sensitivity to make sure that ESL students understand and will be aided in remembering the exchanges made during the conference.

Finally, depending on a host of factors, including the students' ages when they began study of English, how literate they are in their native languages, and how proficient they want to become in English, ESL students will become more or less good writers of English, but it is unlikely that they will become flawless writers or that they will be able to produce flawless texts in English without a great deal of effort. Whether or not they are willing to exert that effort also depends on many variables, including their own goals in learning to write in English, the linguistic distance between English and their native language, and their desire to be regarded primarily as a member of our academic discourse community rather than as a Lebanese, Zairean, or Korean student. But even if they do not become flawless writers of English, their numerous minor errors may be thought of as a kind of foreign accent, only in writing instead of in speech.

Dealing with Grammar

If grammatical errors are going to be addressed, how is this best accomplished by non-ESL teachers? Since the expectations, goals, and past writing experiences of ESL students are different from those of native speakers, the question of how best to respond to errors in their writing may need to be different. Some of the strategies used with native speakers, such as having them read their texts out loud, editing automatically, may not work well with non-natives; on the other hand, since many ESL students learned English through traditional grammar-based methods, non-natives are often more likely to be able to benefit from formal explanations of grammar than native speakers are.

What might be a reasonable approach for non-ESL teachers to take in addressing errors, particularly since ESL students make many sentence-level errors? It is probably useless to try to address every error. Teachers might want to select errors for attention. Stigmatizing errors are good candidates, since these are often the same ones made by native speakers and have traditionally been associated with lack of education: formal conventions of appearance (setting appropriate margins, for example), subject-verb agreements, the occasional misuse of forms that native speakers also misuse (*theirselves* for *themselves*), or sentence boundary errors. If these types of errors cause irritation or stigmatize students, they should probably not simply be left to fade out of a student's interlanguage at their own speed.

Another useful distinction to help teachers decide which errors to address might be between local and global errors (Burt and Kiparsky, 1972). Local errors are those which disturb only a small portion of a text—a missing article, for example, or an incorrect preposition. A global error has a greater effect on understanding and might be, for that reason, considered more "serious" or more appropriate for correction. Global errors may involve incorrect lexical choices but they usually disturb syntax. Burt and Kiparsky give the example of the sentence: *English language use much people*. There are two local errors (*the* English language and *many* people) and one global error, the order of the words. If both of the local errors are corrected (*The English language use many people*), the sentence is still difficult to understand; if just the global error is corrected (*Much people use English language*), the sentence is more acceptable. It seems reasonable that if only some errors are to be corrected, they should be the ones which create the greatest potential misunderstanding.

A more recent trend in error correction proposes differential treatment of errors based not on considerations of error gravity but rather on insight into the language processing strategies that learners use to internalize language input (Gajdusek, 1990). The question to raise is whether the error is part of a rule-governed feature of English or is simply part of English's arbitrary categorizing system, as in countable/uncountable nouns or verb complementation. Response to these two types of errors must differ since no amount of explanation will allow a learner to understand why *assignments* can be plural but *homework* cannot. But the most important feature of an approach which attempts to get at whether an error is part of a teachable/learnable rule-governed system or not is the learner's own interlanguage sense of how English works.

Teachers who would like to help students correct sentence-level errors might begin to get a picture of the students' interlanguage by asking them to explain their reason for constructing a phrase or sentence as they did. Sometimes students have internalized an incorrect version of a grammar rule. If that misunderstanding can be revealed and a correct version of the rule substituted, then even if students cannot produce the correct form spontaneously, they can use the corrected rule to help them edit texts.

If students cannot describe the rule they employed in constructing a particular form, teachers can help students analyze their own understandings of features of English by giving several correct and incorrect versions of the misused structure and having them indicate which uses they feel are correct and which are not. From these choices it may be possible to determine where interlanguage versions of the structure are skewed. Another technique aiming in the same direction is to give students several sentences all containing the same error and to ask them to describe what principle of English is being violated. These techniques help interlanguage structures become explicit to student and teacher alike.

Occasionally, students make errors because features of English are not salient to them; terminal *-s* is a good example. It is usually redundant, carrying no meaning itself not available from surrounding text, and it is often dropped in the pronunciation of many students either because terminal *-s* cannot exist in their language or because terminal *-s* is written but never pronounced. Sometimes dictating a sentence for students to write will reveal which features of English, like terminal *-s*, they do not attend to even when those features are present in the dictated text.

Another technique for helping ESL students get correct input on errors they have made on rule-governed features of English is to write out a standard or correct version of an incorrect form or sentence and then ask them to describe the differences between the correct and the incorrect form. Next, ask students if they can generalize a rule governing the standard use or, better yet, if they can describe what pattern they should look for as they edit other sentences. Finally, ask students to look for other examples of the same usage in their own writing.

Since many ESL students have had training in formal grammar, there is no particular reason not to make use of formal grammar in attempting to clarify interlanguage images of grammatical rules. But these appeals to formal grammar are helpful only if the teacher is conscious of English grammar rules that are problematic *for non-natives*. Unfortunately, the rules and explanations of rules which may be appropriate for native speakers often are not relevant to non-natives. ESL students are sometimes misled by grammar explanations from non-ESL trained teachers or tutors who explain rules that create no particular difficulty for ESL students (*could of done* versus *could have done*), who explain too much of a rule in response to what may have been only a slip in English rather than a real error in understanding, or who explain rules simply by appeal to what sounds right ("We wouldn't say, 'They risked to go into the building.'")

How Far Do We Go?

But most important in considering responses to ESL students' writing errors is the question of how far to go, how native-like their writing must be to be acceptable. In the end, teachers of ESL students need to recognize that they probably cannot cure very many grammar ills with conscious effort, and certainly not in the period of time institutionally designated for that purpose. Furthermore, whether or not a student's writing becomes error-free depends a great deal on the student's desire for error-free work. Some ESL students are content with being communicative and do not care about being seen as integrated into the target community—in this case, the English-speaking academic discourse community. If this is the case, very little grammatical correction will have any effect on reshaping the students' interlanguage forms (Schumann, 1978).

Non-ESL teachers sometimes worry that ESL students will need to be evaluated differently from the way native speakers are evaluated. They worry about lowering standards. Perhaps a more fruitful approach to the question of how much ESL students' texts must resemble those of native speakers might be to develop a broadened definition of good writing. ESL students can become very fluent writers of English, but they may never become indistinguishable from a native speaker, and it is unclear why they should. A current movement among ESL writing teachers is to argue that, beyond a certain level of proficiency in English writing, it is not the students' texts that need to change; rather it is the native-speaking readers and evaluators (particularly in educational institutions) that need to learn to read more broadly, with a more cosmopolitan, less parochial eye. The infusion of life brought by these ESL students' different perspectives on the world can only benefit a pluralistic society which is courageous enough truly to embrace its definition of itself.

very true —
how to make this ? happen.

Conclusion

Becoming proficient in a second language takes time, longer than we once thought, even for young children, who seem to pick up languages so quickly. ESL students are juggling a variety of learning experiences and, especially at the college level, are being asked to perform expertly in a number of areas at the same time. Not only are they dealing with the content of courses in their majors and other subjects—and trying to do this in a foreign language—but they also have to deal with their social environment as adults, find apartments and child care, open bank accounts, deal with medical problems, pay taxes. To all of this burden we can add the pain and loneliness of being away from loved ones and familiar social support systems. Immigrant students may also be dealing with the misery and injustice of racist attitudes and behaviors toward them and their families.

These, then, are the students who enter our writing classrooms. All classrooms are different. The variety of configurations of teachers, pedagogies, course goals, and students in a class make it pointless to attempt to give suggestions about specific assignments that would work for ESL students, or specific pedagogies, or other sorts of specific advice. I hope that a better understanding of ESL students and what they bring with them to our classrooms will set the groundwork for teachers to make informed decisions of their own about what will work best in their particular teaching contexts. The following few general suggestions are offered as beginnings toward making contact with ESL students in our classes, understanding them better, and making their experiences, as well as those of our native students, more positive and stimulating.

The most helpful and positive action we can take as teachers is to get to know ESL students in our classes. We need to take time to talk to them one to one, immediately, on the first or second day of class. Conversations can give teachers an initial sense of how much these students understand, and this may be helpful in planning lectures or class activities. But more importantly, friendly, casual interactions before or after class can give us a sense of who these students are, their backgrounds and goals. But these contacts must be undertaken in a welcoming way, one which does not isolate them by singling them out as different from the other students, as odd, as a problem. An inappropriate, though no doubt well intended, strategy is to call the students aside and let them know that they will have to work hard, that the class may be over their heads, that they will have trouble succeeding. Even if such comments are followed by offers to give extra help, they undermine the students' self-confidence. Most likely, these students are already painfully aware that they are facing additional burdens in classes with native English speakers; they do not need to be reminded.

Consulting with students on their role in the class is an appropriate avenue to explore. ESL teachers so often hear stories of non-native students whose teachers, not really knowing what to do for them in class, simply let them sit there, not participating, not learning. We might instead ask ESL students if they mind being called on in class. Some of them may prefer not to be; our classes may be their first experience with mixed-gender classes, for instance, and they may feel intimidated or embarrassed by the mere presence of members of the other gender. Others will hesitate to participate *unless* specifically called on. We might let them know that, if they are willing, we are eager to turn to them for their own perspectives, or those of their country, on issues that come up in class. They are thus seen by their classmates as experts adding something special to the class, not as quiet oddities to be ignored until they blend into the furniture. Research shows that teachers tend to call on students who are like themselves, ethnically and socio-economically, and therefore do not give the same attention to all students (Scarcella, 1990). We need to make a conscious effort to avoid favoring some groups and ignoring others.

Some students may need a period of non-participation before they feel comfortable enough to talk in front of a whole class. This is where small group work can be especially beneficial, making them feel comfortable speaking first with a limited number of students whom they get to know before having to speak publicly.

We can also encourage friendly relations between ESL and native English-speaking students by asking a specific native student (again, before or after class) to help an international student with something, anything, finding the library or perhaps sharing class notes.

Class formats can work to incorporate or exclude students as well. Lecture-style classes may be especially difficult for non-native students, since teachers may lecture too fast and in too colloquial a style for ESL students to follow easily. Slowing down and speaking more carefully, especially at the beginning of a term, does not seem too great a concession to make to non-natives in our classes. Even among native speakers, students have different learning styles. Adherence to one single class format is inadvisable in any case since it works to the detriment of those who learn better in other ways. All students deserve to be treated with sensitivity and consideration.

For writing teachers, one form that sensitivity can take is in making writing assignments. Certain topics pose particular complications for ESL students. Whether writing topics are assigned by the teacher or student selected, it makes sense to consult with ESL students about writing topics to determine their suitability.

Finally, as we saw in Chapter 7, ESL students need more time than their native English-speaking classmates to complete the same tasks. No magic number of assignments completed or words written in themselves confirm that a student has learned the course material or developed the requisite amount of writing skill to successfully pass a course. There is no getting around the fact that ESL students must work harder and longer on writing assignments than native students do, and there seems to be no reason to insist that they carry that extra burden. Surely, it is the quality of the work that matters and not the quantity.

The challenge ESL students face is immense. Whether they are international students or immigrant students, entering our universities means entering into competition in the domain of language against others who are natural experts. While native students may know no more about calculus than these students, while they may have spent the same number of years as ESL students have in trying to master chemical equations, while they too may be new to the higher educational setting, native students have spent all their lives interacting in English and have been formally trained in reading and writing in English for at least twelve years by the time they reach their freshman college year. For some of the international students, English may be only a year or two old. Others may have had a disinterested contact with English two to four hours a week for four years in high school. These students' mission of graduating from a U.S. institution seems almost heroic in this light. Add to the difficulty of competing in an English-speaking environment the wrenching sadness of personal sacrifice and the real deprivation of financial sacrifice and it is a wonder that so many of these students survive at all.

A great part of their survival comes at least in part from the personal contacts or relationships they are able to establish here.

Given how much we can learn and need to learn about the lives of other human beings around the world, it is clear that we can make the lives of non-native students easier and our own richer by trying to understand and interact with them. My intention throughout this book has been to contribute in some way to making that comfort and wealth more possible.

Notes

Chapter Two

1. The Guiora et al. (1972) study showed the positive effects of alcohol (up to a point!) on language production. People who drank a shot before class performed better than those who had no alcohol or too much.

Chapter Three

1. The distinction I am trying to draw here is between ESL students, who are neither native speakers nor bilingual English speakers, and SESD students, who are native or bilingual speakers of English but who do not have facility with standard written English (SWE). Ways of designating this second category of students change, but at the moment among ESL professionals, the term SESD is being used. To some extent these language-minority students are probably also what Cummins (1979) refers to as BICS, those proficient in Basic Interpersonal Communication Skills but less familiar with the privileged dialect of schools and the academy. SESD students may certainly include immigrants to English-speaking countries, while ESL students, for the purposes of this discussion, are likely to be international or visa students who seek education in an English-speaking country but have probably completed high school in their home countries.

2. Some debate exists about exactly how much of the writing skill which one develops in a first language is then directly transferable to a second language (Jones and Tetroe, 1987; Jones, 1985). In other words, even if ESL students write well in L1, there may be restrictions on how fully they may be able to draw upon those skills in L2.

3. On the other hand, the Santos study shows that faculty rate lexical errors as the most serious errors. This suggests that errors which interfere with meaning are the most irritating and least acceptable, a conclusion which the Vann et al. study corroborates.

4. Teachers of English to Speakers of Other Languages, the international professional organization of ESL and EFL teachers.

5. It is not clear whether these ESL students were also basic writers or whether they were simply inexperienced with English.

Chapter Six

1. Some students from cultures which do not normally value personal discovery writing may find this type of writing liberating. Ironically, it may be precisely because this writing takes place in the L2 that it is perceived positively. In a sense, writing in the L2 does not feel real, just as swearing in an L2 carries much less impact than it does in the L1. In other words, even if the students are not inventing details of their lives in personal discovery writing, in a sense they are. They are still fabricating. Writing in L1 is real. Writing in L2 lacks reality; it is daydreaming, pretending, writing once-removed.

2. See Kroll (1988) for a discussion of native students' attitudes toward plagiarism.

Chapter Seven

1. It should be noted, however, that increased proficiency in L2 benefited average writers more than it did either experienced or basic writers, although the effect was still additive rather than indicative of qualitative changes in students' thinking about writing (Cumming, 1989).

2. Evidence from reading research suggests that there is a threshold of L2 proficiency which a learner must have attained in order to be able to make use of good L1 reading strategies (Clarke, 1979). In other words, beginning learners of English who are good readers in their L1s cannot make use of those good reading strategies until they have advanced in their English proficiency. However, Hudson (1982) points out that, just as L2 proficiency can limit the use of good L1 reading strategies, good L1 reading strategies can limit the restrictive effects of lack of L2 proficiency; these two elements, language proficiency and good reading strategies, share a symbiotic relationship.

For writing, it is not clear how a linguistic threshold might function, however, since not enough research on writing has addressed beginning language learners. An essential difference between reading and writing, especially for the L2 learner, is that in writing the learner controls the language whereas in reading the learner must deal with whatever language appears in the text. As a result, writing at these beginning stages may actually be easier than reading, however counter-intuitive that may seem.

The question of L2 reading is beyond the scope of this book. Furthermore, most writing teachers are not also reading teachers and are busy enough simply addressing writing problems. But the connection between reading and writing ability is as pertinent in L2 as it is in L1 (see Carson and Leki, forthcoming).

3. All page-number cites are to the pre-publication manuscript.

4. Campbell (1990) finds this insecurity expressed in another domain. In a summary writing assignment, the L2 writers she studied were more dependent on the original text than were the L1 writers. Her L2 students

may have felt they could not presume to write better than what was already written or they may simply not have known other options for expressing the ideas in the original text.

Chapter Eight

1. In a survey of seventy-seven international students, Liebman-Kleine (1986) also reports that these students remember studying writing in school and, interestingly, being told to write in patterns similar to what they later learned is the appropriate pattern to use in English. These students reported that their school teachers had told them good writing had an introduction, development with support, and a conclusion. But it is possible that the students were merely projecting their current familiarity with English writing patterns into the past.

2. Thus, the status of errors in rhetoric is similar to that of errors in socio-linguistic patterns of thanking or apologizing. Native speakers adapt fairly easily to spoken accents but are likely to take failure to say thank you or to apologize according to expected English norms as a personal affront or as boorishness on the part of the non-native speaker rather than seeing these errors as evidence of an imperfect command over English, in the same way a foreign accent is viewed (Wolfson, 1989). The non-native who makes a socio-linguistic error is viewed as boorish and the one who makes a rhetorical error is viewed as illogical.

Chapter Nine

1. It is not entirely clear which kinds of ESL errors content faculty find most irritating and least acceptable. While professors in the Santos study were especially critical of errors which native students also make, other studies show a somewhat different picture. In one study of faculty reaction to writing errors by non-native students, faculty most readily accepted two kinds of errors: (1) spelling, comma splice, and pronoun agreement errors of the type native speakers would also make and (2) article and preposition errors, which native speakers would not make but which were presumably regarded as tricky areas for non-natives. They were more critical of certain other types of errors which native speakers would not usually make and which would be considered language learner errors. The researchers' explanation is that this last category of errors, those which only L2 learners would be likely to make, disturbed comprehension of the message and, therefore, were considered the least tolerable (Vann, Meyer, and Lorenz, 1984).

There is also the suggestion among researchers (Albrechtsen, Henriksen, and Faerch, 1980) that, in fact, the *type* of error is of little consequence. All errors are irritating, and what counts is the number, not the type, of errors. In other words, readers can tolerate a certain number of any type of error more or less equally. What they cannot tolerate is a large number of errors, regardless of how otherwise inconsequential they might be.

2. The Fathman and Whalley study (1990) showed that feedback on errors produced better subsequent drafts *of the same paper*. Feedback on content also produced better subsequent drafts, but the improvement was not as great as the improvement in form had been. These findings might be interpreted as showing that improving form is easier than improving content, at least in the same paper. Other interesting findings from this study indicate (1) that no feedback at all on content also produced improvement of content, (2) that no feedback either on form or on content resulted in longer essays, and (3) that feedback on content and form could appear at the same time on the same draft with no negative effect on the amount of improvement. This last finding suggests that it is unnecessary to separate out feedback on content for one draft and hold off feedback on form for a subsequent draft.

3. An asterisk before a sentence or phrase indicates a non-standard form.

4. To get an idea of the wide grammatical divergence between English and another language, from the point of view of syntax alone, consider these two examples (Kim, 1988) from English and Korean:

English: *Although I told Sookja not to hit the dog, she hit it.*

Word for word translation of the same idea from Korean: *I Sookja the dog hit not told although hit.* (262)

Bibliography

Albrechtsen, D., B. Henriksen, and C. Faerch. 1980. Native speaker reactions to learners' spoken interlanguage. *Language Learning* 30:365–396.

Andersen, R., ed. 1983. *Pidginization and creolization as language acquisition*. Rowley, MA: Newbury House.

Arndt, V. 1987. Six writers in search of texts: A protocol-based study of L1 and L2 writing. *ELT Journal* 41:257–267.

Bailey, N., C. Madden, and S. Krashen. 1974. Is there a natural sequence in adult second language acquisition? *Language Learning* 24:235–243.

Bander, R. G. 1971. *American English rhetoric*. New York: Holt, Rinehart, and Winston.

Bartholomae, D. 1980. Study of error. *College Composition and Communication* 31:253–269.

Bassetti, C. 1990. How do students coming from a French schooling system adapt themselves to the American composition style? Unpublished manuscript.

Belenky, M., B. M. Clinchy, N. R. Goldberger, and J. M. Tarule. 1986. *Women's ways of knowing*. New York: Basic Books.

Benesch, S. 1991. *ESL in America: Myths and possibilities*. Portsmouth, NH: Boynton/Cook.

Benson, M., E. Benson, and R. Ilson. 1986. *BBI combinatory dictionary of English: A guide to word combinations*. Philadelphia: John Benjamin Publishing.

Bereiter, C. and M. Scardamalia. 1987. *The psychology of written composition*. Hillsdale, NJ: Lawrence Erlbaum.

Biber, D. 1988. *Variation across speech and writing*. New York: Cambridge.

Bickner, R. and P. Peyasantiwong. 1988. Cultural variation in reflective writing. In *Writing across languages and cultures*, ed. A. Purves. Newbury Park, CA: Sage.

Braddock, R. 1974. The frequency and placement of topic sentences in expository prose. *Research in the Teaching of English* 8:287–302.

Brannon, L. and C. H. Knoblauch. 1982. On students' rights to their own texts: A model of teacher response. *College Composition and Communication* 33:157–166.

Brodkey, D. 1983. An expectancy exercise in cohesion. *TESL Reporter* 16:43–45.

Brown, H. D. 1980. *Principles of language learning and teaching.* Englewood Cliffs, NJ: Prentice-Hall.

Bruder, M. N. and L. Hayden. 1973. Teaching composition: A report on a bidialectal approach. *Language Learning* 23:1−15.

Burkland, J. and N. Grimm. 1986. Motivating through responding. *Journal of Teaching Writing* 5:237−247.

Burt, M. 1975. Error analysis in the adult EFL classroom. *TESOL Quarterly* 9:53−63.

Burt, M. and C. Kiparsky. 1972. *The gooficon.* Rowley, MA: Newbury House.

Burtoff, M. 1983. The logical organization of written expository discourse in English: A comparative study of Japanese, Arabic, and native speaker strategies. Unpublished doctoral dissertation, Georgetown Univ.

Butler, J. 1980. Remedial writers: The teacher's job as corrector of papers. *College Composition and Communication* 31:270−277.

Campbell, C. 1990. Writing with others' words: Using background reading text in academic compositions. In *Second language writing,* ed. B. Kroll. New York: Cambridge.

Carrell, P. 1984. The effects of rhetorical organization on ESL readers. *TESOL Quarterly* 18:441−469.

――――. 1983. Three components of background knowledge in reading comprehension. *Language Learning* 33:183−205.

Carrell, P. and J. C. Eisterhold. 1983. Schema theory and ESL reading pedagogy. *TESOL Quarterly* 17:553−573.

Carroll, J. and S. Sapon. 1958. *Modern Language Aptitude Test.* New York: The Psychological Corporation.

Carson, I. and I. Leki. Forthcoming. *Reading in the composition classroom: Second language perspectives.* Boston: Newbury House.

Caudill, H. M. 1963. *Night comes to the Cumberlands.* Boston: Little, Brown.

Clarke, M. A. 1979. Reading in Spanish and English: Evidence from adult ESL students. *Language Learning* 29:121−150.

Clyne, M. G. 1984. English and German. In *Annual review of applied linguistics 3,* ed. R. Kaplan. Rowley, MA: Newbury House.

Cohen, A. and M. C. Cavalcanti. 1990. Feedback on compositions: Teacher and student verbal reports. In *Second language writing,* ed. B. Kroll. New York: Cambridge.

Collado, A. V. 1981. Using the students' first language: Comparing and contrasting. *HEIS Newsletter* 3(September):9−10.

Connor, U. 1984. Recall of text: Differences between first and second language readers. *TESOL Quarterly* 18:239−256.

Connor, U. and M. Farmer. 1990. The teaching of topical structure analysis as a revision strategy: An exploratory study. In *Second language writing,* ed. B. Kroll. New York: Cambridge.

Connor, U. and R. Kaplan. 1987. *Writing across languages: Analysis of L2 text*. Reading, MA: Addison-Wesley.

Connor, U. and P. McCagg. 1983. Cross-cultural differences and perceived quality in written paraphrases of English expository prose. *Applied Linguistics* 4:259−268.

Cowan, J. W. 1978. Factors influencing Arab and Iranian students in-country and in the U.S. In *Students from the Arab world and Iran*, ed. G. Althen. Washington: NAFSA.

Cumming, A. 1989. Writing expertise and second language proficiency. *Language Learning* 39:81−141.

Cummins, J. 1979. Linguistic interdependence and the educational development of bilingual children. *Review of Educational Research* 49:222−251.

Davies, E. E. 1985. Communication as a criterion for error evaluation. *International Review of Applied Linguistics* 23:65−69.

Dennett, J. T. 1990. ESL technical writing: Process and rhetorical difference. Paper presented at the Conference of College Composition and Communication, Chicago.

Dulay, H. C. and M. K. Burt. 1974. Natural sequences in child second language acquisition. *Language Learning* 24:37−53.

Edamatsu, F. 1978. The Japanese psycho-social barrier in learning English. *TESL Reporter* 12(Fall):4−6, 17−19.

Eggington, W. G. 1987. Written academic discourse in Korean: Implications for effective communication. In *Writing across languages: Analysis of L2 text*, eds. U. Connor and R. Kaplan. Reading, MA: Addison-Wesley.

Ellis, R. 1985. *Understanding second language acquisition*. New York: Oxford.

Eskey, D. E. 1983. Meanwhile, back in the real world . . . : Accuracy and fluency in second language teaching. *TESOL Quarterly* 17:315−323.

Faigley, L. 1989. Judging writing, judging selves. *College Composition and Communication* 40:395−412.

Fathman, A. K. and E. Whalley. 1990. Teacher treatment of error: Focus on form versus content. In *Second language writing*, ed. B. Kroll. New York: Cambridge.

Finocchiaro, M. 1974. *English as a second language: From theory to practice*. New York: Regents.

Freedman, A., I. Pringle, and J. Yalden, eds. 1983. *Learning to write: First language/second language*. New York: Longman.

Friedlander, A. 1990. Composing in English: Effects of a first language on writing in English in a second language. In *Second language writing*, ed. B. Kroll. New York: Cambridge.

Fries, C. C. 1945. Teaching and learning English as a foreign language. Ann Arbor: University of Michigan Press.

Gajdusek, L. 1990. Responding to written errors: Respecting process, teaching language. Paper presented at TESOL Conference, San Francisco.

Gardner, R. and W. Lambert. 1972. *Attitudes and motivation in second language learning.* Rowley, MA: Newbury House.

Gordon, B. 1987. Another look: Standardized tests for placement in college composition courses. *WPA: Writing Program Administration* 10:29–38.

Grabe, W. and R. Kaplan. 1989. Writing in a second language: Contrastive rhetoric. In *Richness in writing: Empowering ESL students,* eds. D. Johnson and D. Roen. New York: Longman.

Guiora, A., B. Beit-Hallami, R. Brannon, C. Dull, and T. Scovel. 1972. The effects of experimentally induced changes in ego states on pronunciation ability in second language: An exploratory study. *Comprehensive Psychiatry* 13:421–428.

Guiora, A., R. Brannon, and C. Dull. 1972. Empathy and second-language learning. *Language Learning* 22:111–130.

Hairston, M. 1982. The winds of change: Thomas Kuhn and the revolution in the teaching of writing. *College Composition and Communication* 33(1):76–88.

Hall, C. 1990. Managing the complexity of revising across languages. *TESOL Quarterly* 24:43–60.

Hamp-Lyons, L. 1986. No new lamps for old yet, please. *TESOL Quarterly* 20(4):790–796.

Hatch, E., P. Polin, and S. Part. 1970. Acoustic scanning or syntactic processing. Paper presented at meeting of Western Psychological Association, San Francisco.

Havens, K. L. 1989. A study in the different responses to error corrections of ESL and SESD writers. Unpublished manuscript.

Hinds, J. 1987. Reader vs writer responsibility: A new typology. In *Writing across languages: Analysis of L2 text,* eds. U. Connor and R. Kaplan. Reading, MA: Addison-Wesley.

———. 1980. Japanese expository prose. *Papers in Linguistics* 13:117–158.

Hirsch, E. D., J. Kett, and J. Trefil. 1988. *The dictionary of cultural literacy.* Boston: Houghton Mifflin.

Hornsby, A. S. 1983. *Oxford students' dictionary of American English.* London: Oxford.

Horowitz, D. 1986a. Essay examination prompts and the teaching of academic writing. *English for Specific Purposes* 5(2):107–120.

———. 1986b. Process, not product: Less than meets the eye. *TESOL Quarterly* 20:141–144.

———. 1986c. What professors actually require: Academic tasks for the ESL classroom. *TESOL Quarterly* 20:445–462.

Huckin, T. and L. Olsen. 1984. The need for professionally oriented ESL instruction in the U.S. *TESOL Quarterly* 18(2):273−294.

Hudson, T. 1982. The effects of induced schemata on the "short circuit" in L2 reading: Non-decoding factors in L2 reading performance. *Language Learning* 32:1−31.

Jenkins, S. and J. Hinds. 1987. Business letter writing: English, French, and Japanese. *TESOL Quarterly* 21:327−349.

Jie, G. and M. J. Lederman. 1988. Instruction and assessment of writing in China: The national unified entrance examination for institutions of higher education. *Journal of Basic Writing* 7:47−60.

Johns, A. 1991. English for specific purposes (ESP): Its history and contributions. In *Teaching English as a second or foreign language*, 2nd edition, ed. M. Celce-Murcia. New York: Newbury House, pp. 67−77.

Johnson, C. 1985. The composing process of six ESL students. *Dissertation Abstracts International* 46(5):121A.

Johnson, D. M. and D. H. Roen. 1989. *Richness in writing: Empowering ESL students.* New York: Longman.

Jones, S. 1985. Problems with monitor use in second language composing. In *When a writer can't write*, ed. M. Rose. New York: Guilford Press.

Jones, S. and J. Tetroe. 1987. Composing in a second language. In *Writing in real time*, ed. A. Matsuhashi. New York: Longman.

Joos, M. 1961. *The five clocks: A linguistic excursion into the five styles of English usage.* New York: Harcourt, Brace, and World, Inc.

Kachru, Y. 1984. English and Hindi. In *Annual review of applied linguistics* 3, ed. R. Kaplan. Rowley, MA: Newbury House.

Kaplan, R. 1988. Contrastive rhetoric and second language learning: Notes toward a theory of contrastive rhetoric. In *Writing across languages and cultures*, ed. A. Purves. Newbury Park, CA: Sage.

———. 1966. Cultural thought patterns in inter-cultural education. *Language Learning* 16:1−20.

Kessler, C., J. Heflin, and F. Fasano. 1982. Psycho-social dynamics in second language acquisition: A case study of Vietnamese brothers. *Proceedings of the Los Angeles second language research forum* 2:144−157.

Kim, B.-L. 1988. The language situation of Korean Americans. In *Language diversity, problem or resource?*, eds. S. McKay and S.-L. C. Wong. Rowley, MA: Newbury House.

Kobayashi, H. 1984. Rhetorical patterns in English and Japanese. *Dissertation Abstracts International* 45(8):2425A.

Krapels, A. R. 1990. An overview of second language writing process research. In *Second language writing*, ed. B. Kroll. New York: Cambridge.

Krashen, S. 1984. *Writing: Research, theory, and applications.* New York: Pergamon Institute.

———. 1982. *Principles and practice in second language acquisition.* New York: Pergamon Press.

———. 1981. *Second language acquisition and second language learning.* New York: Pergamon Press.

———. 1973. Lateralization, language learning and the critical period: Some new evidence. *Language Learning* 23:63–74.

Krashen, S. and T. Terrell. 1983. *The natural approach.* Oxford: Pergamon.

Krasnick, H. 1990. Preparing Indonesians for graduate study in Canada. *TESL Reporter* 23:33–36.

Kroll, Barbara. 1991. Teaching writing in the ESL context. In *Teaching English as a second or foreign language,* 2nd edition, ed. M. Celce-Murcia. New York: Newbury House.

———. 1990. *Second language writing.* New York: Cambridge.

Kroll, Barry. 1988. How college freshmen view plagiarism. *Written Communication* 5:203–221.

Kuehn, P., D. J. Stanwick, and C. L. Holland. 1990. Attitudes toward "cheating" behaviors in the ESL classroom. *TESOL Quarterly* 24:313–317.

Lamendella, J. 1979. The neurofunctional basis of pattern practice. *TESOL Quarterly* 13:5–19.

Land, R. and C. Whitley. 1989. Evaluating second language essays in regular composition classes: Toward a pluralistic U.S. rhetoric. In *Richness in writing: Empowering ESL students,* eds. D. M. Johnson and D. H. Roen. New York: Longman.

Larsen, D. A. and W. A. Smalley. 1972. *Becoming bilingual.* New Canaan, Conn: Practical Anthropology.

Larsen-Freeman, D. and M. Long. 1991. *Introduction to second language acquisition research.* New York: Longman.

Lay, N. 1982. Composing processes of adult ESL learners: A case study. *TESOL Quarterly* 16:406.

Leki, I. 1991a. Twenty-five years of contrastive rhetoric: Text analysis and writing pedagogies. *TESOL Quarterly* 25:123–143.

———. 1991b. Preferences of ESL students for error correction in college-level writing classes. *Foreign Language Annals* 24(3):203–218.

———. 1990a. Coaching from the margins: Issues in written response. In *Second language writing,* ed. B. Kroll. New York: Cambridge.

———. 1990b. Potential problems with peer responding in ESL writing classes. *CATESOL Journal* 3:5–19.

Leki, I. and R. Wallace. 1988. Cultural literacy: An ESL mission or a mission impossible? Paper presented at Conference on Reading, Literacy, and Culture, Atlanta.

Lenneberg, E. 1967. *Biological foundations of language.* New York: Wiley and Sons.

Levine, R. with E. Wolff. 1985. Social time: The heartbeat of a culture. *Psychology Today* 19(March):28–37.

Lewis, T. and R. Jungman, eds. 1986. *On being foreign: Culture shock in short fiction.* Yarmouth, Maine: Intercultural Press.

Liebman-Kleine, J. 1988. Contrastive rhetoric: Students as ethnographers. *Journal of Basic Writing* 7(2):6−27.

——. 1986a. In defense of teaching process in ESL composition. *TESOL Quarterly* 20(4):783−788.

——. 1986b. Towards a contrastive new rhetoric−a rhetoric of process. ERIC Document 271963.

Lightbown, P. 1985. Great expectations: Second-language acquisition research and classroom teaching. *Applied Linguistics* 6:173−189.

MacDonald, M. G. and C. Hall. 1990. Doctoral-level teacher training in ESL writing. Paper presented at Southeast Regional TESOL Conference, Louisville, KY.

McKay, S. L. 1989. Topic development and written discourse accent. In *Richness in writing: Empowering ESL students*, eds. D. Johnson and D. Roen. New York: Longman.

McKay, S. and S.-L. C. Wong, eds. 1988. *Language diversity, problem or resource?* Rowley, MA: Newbury House.

McLaughlin, B. 1987. *Theories of second language learning.* London: Edward Arnold.

McLeod, B. and B. McLaughlin. 1986. Restructuring or automatization: Reading in a second language. *Language Learning* 36:109−126.

Matalene, C. 1985. Contrastive rhetoric: An American writing teacher in China. *College English* 47:789−808.

Mohan, B. A. and W. A.-Y. Lo. 1985. Academic writing and Chinese students: Transfer and developmental factors. *TESOL Quarterly* 19:515−534.

Murray, D. E. 1989. Teaching the bilingual writer. In *The writing teacher's manual*, ed. H. P. Guth. Belmont, CA: Wadsworth.

Naiman, N., M. Frohlich, H. Stern, and A. Todesco. 1978. *The good language learner. Research in education No. 7.* Toronto: Ontario Institute for Studies in Education.

Nattinger, J. 1978. Second dialect and second language in the composition class. *TESOL Quarterly* 12:77−84.

Nelson, M. W. 1991. *At the point of need: Teaching basic and ESL writers.* Portsmouth, NH: Boynton/Cook.

Newstetter, W., T. Shoji, N. Mokoto, and F. Matsubara. 1989. From the inside out: Student perspectives on the academic writing culture. Paper presented at the Conference on Culture, Writing, and Related Issues in Language Teaching, Atlanta.

O'Connor, F. 1961. Everything that rises must converge. In *Exploring literature through reading and writing*, eds. B. Drabeck, H. Ellis, and H. Pfeil. Boston: Houghton Mifflin.

Oliver, R. 1971. *Communication and culture in ancient India and China.* Syracuse, NY: Syracuse University Press.

Ostler, S. 1987. English in parallels: A comparison of English and Arabic prose. In *Writing across languages: Analysis of L2 text*, eds. U. Connor and R. Kaplan. Reading, MA: Addison-Wesley.

Paulston, C. B. and G. Dykstra. 1973. *Controlled composition in English as a second language*. New York: Regents.

Penfield, W. and L. Roberts. 1959. *Speech and brain mechanisms*. New York: Atheneum Press.

Perl, S. 1979. The composing processes of unskilled college writers. *Research in the Teaching of English* 13:317−336.

Perry, W. 1981. Cognitive and ethical growth. In *The modern American college*, ed. A. E. Chickering. San Francisco: Jossey-Bass.

Piaget, J. 1968. *Six psychological studies*. Translation by Anita Elkind. New York: Vintage Books.

Proctor, P., ed. 1987. *Longman dictionary of contemporary English*. New York: Longman.

Prothro, E. T. 1955. Arab-American differences in the judgment of written messages. *Journal of Social Psychology* 42:3−11.

Purves, A. 1988. *Writing across languages and cultures: Issues in contrastive rhetoric*. Newbury Park, CA: Sage.

Radecki, P. M. and J. Swales. 1988. ESL students' reaction to written comments on their written work. *System* 16:355−365.

Raimes, A. 1985. What unskilled writers do as they write: A classroom study. *TESOL Quarterly* 19:229−258.

─────. 1984. Anguish as a second language? Remedies for composition teachers. In *Composing in a second language*, ed. S. McKay. Rowley, MA: Newbury House.

Reid, J. 1989. English as a second language composition in higher education: The expectations of the academic audience. In *Richness in writing: Empowering ESL students*, eds. D. Johnson and D. Roen. NY: Longman.

Rivers, W. 1968. Teaching foreign language skills. Chicago: University of Chicago Press.

Robb, T., S. Ross, and I. Shortreed. 1986. Salience of Feedback on error and its effect on EFL writing quality. *TESOL Quarterly* 20:83−95.

Rose, M. 1989. *Lives on the Boundary: The struggles and achievements of America's underprepared*. New York: Penguin.

Roy, A. 1984. Alliance for literacy: Teaching non-native speakers and speakers of non-standard English together. *College Composition and Communication* 35:439−448.

Sachs, J. 1967. Recognition memory for syntactic and semantic aspects of connected discourse. *Perception and Psychophysics* 2:437−442.

Santos, T. 1988. Professors' reactions to the academic writing of non-native speaking students. *TESOL Quarterly* 22:69−90.

Savignon, S. 1972. *Communicative competence: An experiment in foreign language teaching*. Philadelphia: The Center for Curriculum

Development.

Scarcella, R. 1990. *Teaching language minority children in the multicultural classroom.* Englewood Cliffs, NJ: Prentice-Hall.

————. 1984. How writers orient their readers in expository essays: A comparative study of native and non-native English writers. *TESOL Quarterly* 18:671–688.

Schachter, J. 1974. An error in error analysis. *Language Learning* 24:205–214.

Schlumberger, A. and K. Mangelsdorf. 1989. Reading the context. Paper presented at TESOL Conference, San Antonio.

Schumann, J. 1978. Second language acquisition: The pidginization hypothesis. In *Second language acquisition*, ed. E. Hatch. Rowley, MA: Newbury House.

Seliger, H. 1983. Learner interaction in the classroom and its effect on language acquisition. In *Classroom oriented research in second language acquisition*, eds. H. Seliger and M. Long. Rowley, MA: Newbury House.

Selinker, L. 1972. Interlanguage. *International Review of Applied Linguistics* 10:209–231.

Selinker, L. and J. Lamendella. 1978. Two perspectives on fossilization in interlanguage learning. *Interlanguage Studies Bulletin* 3:143–191.

Shaunessy, M. 1977. *Errors and expectations.* New York: Oxford.

Shen, F. 1989. The classroom and the wider culture: Identity as a key to learning English composition. *College Composition and Communication* 40:459–466.

Silva, T. Forthcoming. L1 vs L2 writing: Graduate students' perceptions. *TESL Canada.*

————. 1990. ESL composition instruction: Developments, issues, and directions. In *Second language writing*, ed. B. Kroll. New York: Cambridge.

————. 1989. A critical review of ESL composing process research. Paper presented at TESOL Conference, San Antonio.

Sindlinger, M. P. 1981. You can lead a hose to water but … (More evidence supporting the Monitor Theory). Unpublished master's thesis. Arizona State University.

Skinner, B. F. 1957. *Verbal behavior.* New York: Appleton Century Crofts.

Smith, D. M. 1972. Some implications for the social status of pidgin languages. In *Sociolinguistics in cross-cultural analyses*, eds. P. Smith and R. Shuy. Washington, D.C.: Georgetown University Press.

Spack, R. forthcoming. Student meets text, text meets student: Finding a way into academic discourse. In *Reading in the writing classroom: Second language perspectives*, eds. J. Carson and I. Leki. Boston: Newbury House.

————. 1988. Initiating ESL students into the academic discourse community: How far should we go? *TESOL Quarterly* 22(1):29–52.

Sperling, M. and S. W. Freedman. 1987. A good girl writes like a good girl. *Written Communication* 4:343−369.

Stapleton, S. 1990. From the roller coaster to the round table: Smoothing rough relationships between foreign students and faculty members. *TESL Reporter* 23(April):23−25.

Strong, M., ed. 1988. *Language learning and deafness.* New York: Cambridge.

Swan, M. and B. Smith, eds. 1988. *Learner English: A teacher's guide to interference and other problems.* New York: Cambridge.

Thompson-Panos, K. and M. Thomas-Ruzic. 1983. The least you should know about Arabic: Implications for the ESL writing instructor. *TESOL Quarterly* 17:609−621.

Vann, R. J., D. E. Meyer, and F. O. Lorenz. 1984. Error gravity: A study of faculty opinion of ESL errors. *TESOL Quarterly* 18:427−440.

Weissberg, R. C. 1984. Given and new: Paragraph development models from scientific English. *TESOL Quarterly* 18:485−500.

Widdowson, H. G. 1983. New starts and different kinds of failure. In *Learning to write: First language/second language,* eds. A. Freedman, I. Pringle, and J. Yalden. New York: Longman.

Winterowd, W. R. 1983. From classroom practice into psycholinguist theory. In *Learning to write: First language/second language,* eds. A. Freedman, I. Pringle, and J. Yalden. New York: Longman.

Wolfson, N. 1989. *Perspectives: Sociolinguistics and TESOL.* New York: Newbury House.

Yorkey, R. 1977. Practical EFL techniques for teaching Arabic-speaking students. In *The human factors in ESL,* eds. J. Alatis and R. Crymes, Washington: TESOL.

Zamel, V. 1985. Responding to student writing. *TESOL Quarterly* 19:79−101.

———. 1983. The composing processes of advanced ESL students: Six case studies. *TESOL Quarterly* 17:165−187.

———. 1982. Writing: The process of discovering meaning. *TESOL Quarterly* 16:195−209.

———. 1976. Teaching composition in the ESL classroom: What we can learn from research in the teaching of English. *TESOL Quarterly* 10(1):67−76.

Zellermayer, M. 1988. An analysis of oral and literate texts: Two types of reader-writer relationships in Hebrew and English. In *The social construction of written communication,* eds. B. A. Rafoth and D. L. Rubin. Norwood, NJ: Ablex.